Shut Up and Eat!

tales of chicken, children, and chardonnay

Kathy Buckworth

KEY PORTER  BOOKS

Library and Archives Canada Cataloguing in Publication

Buckworth, Kathy
    Shut up and eat : tales of chicken, children and chardonnay / Kathy Buckworth.

ISBN 978-1-55470-280-0

1. Mothers—Humor. 2. Dinners and dining—Humor. 3. Communication in
Families—Humor. 4. Parenting—Humor. 5. Families—Humor. I. Title.

HQ759.B823 2010   306.874'3   C2009-905894-4

 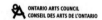

The publisher gratefully acknowledges the support of the Canada Council for the Arts and
the Ontario Arts Council for its publishing program. We acknowledge the support of the
Government of Ontario through the Ontario Media Development Corporation's Ontario
Book Initiative.

We acknowledge the financial support of the Government of Canada through the Book
Publishing Industry Development Program (BPIDP) for our publishing activities.

Key Porter Books Limited
Six Adelaide Street East, Tenth Floor
Toronto, Ontario
Canada M5C 1H6

www.keyporter.com

Text design and electronic formatting: Marijke Friesen
Printed and bound in Canada
10 11 12 13 14 5 4 3 2 1

Mixed Sources
Product group from well-managed
forests, controlled sources and
recycled wood or fiber
www.fsc.org Cert no. SW-COC-002358
© 1996 Forest Stewardship Council
FSC

ANCIENT FOREST ™
FRIENDLY

To all the moms who've ever asked themselves the question,
"What the hell am I going to make for dinner tonight?"

Contents

Part I
Family Meals

Part II
Entertaining

Part III
Take It Easy

Acknowledgements and Apologies

First of all, my apologies to the Society for the Easily Offended for using *shut up* right there in my title. Offended mothers, please avert your eyes. Next to getting your child to sleep, getting your child to eat is one of the most frustrating parts of parenthood— well, not counting the sex, drugs, and other assorted illegal activities they'll get into later. But during the course of writing this book, and endlessly droning on about it, I discovered that it's not just kids who can drive us crazy with their weird eating habits. It's husbands, dinner-party guests, people in restaurants, maybe even your best friend. And so the book grew. And grew.

On a related note, I should apologize right upfront to all of the people who've had the misfortune and misadventure to eat at my house and who haven't behaved exactly as I would have liked them to. Cuz you're in here. And my family? Sorry, but you're all over this. But you're used to me by now, right?

I need to acknowledge my own mom, Gillian Buckworth, who fed four of us—and yes, Mom, I know I was the pickiest eater and you could fill a book with stories about me too—and who managed to somehow turn out (mostly) fully functioning members of society. Coming from England, we got to enjoy many favourites—including roast beef, Yorkshire pudding, and overcooked broccoli (no offence, Mom, I know it's a tradition in your land). Also a nod to my Dad, John Buckworth, who is so devoted to the manly art of barbecuing that when we lived in Winnipeg for 11 long, cold years, he used to crank up the round, red, charcoal BBQ in our garage. For some people 40 below may be too cold for outdoor cooking, but we couldn't miss our Saturday night grilled steak.

I also need to acknowledge my own brood—Steve, Victoria, Alex, Bridget, and Nic—for making it through so many culinary catastrophes with me.

And, as always, to the fantastic folks at Key Porter—my Eager Editor Linda Pruessen, P.R. Princess Kelly Ward, Marketing Mogul Daniel Rondeau, and S&M Master Tom Best. Thanks for still taking my calls.

Also thanks to my agent, Carolyn Swayze, who continues to keep me in her lineup of otherwise real writers.

My peeps, my Tweeps, and everyone in between—you're the best.

Shut Up and Eat!

Introduction
What Fresh Hell Is This?

"Food is an important part of a balanced diet."
—Fran Lebowitz

Feeding your family. It's one of life's biggest challenges, and—in the quintessential Mom world of give and take—also one of life's biggest disappointments. Daily. Let's review this apparent paradox. First, the challenge: Mealtime is a challenge to *you*, busy moms, because finding something to put on the table that is nutritious and delicious and can be made without the prerequisite of a degree from a culinary arts institution is not easy. That's an understatement, actually; it's impossible.

Now to the disappointment: It is inevitable that, despite your best efforts, your family will hate whatever you serve up. Your kids will turn up their noses and declare it inedible. And your husband will point out that you barely came within a glancing blow of *Canada's Food Guide*. (Note: Apparently ketchup is not listed as a vegetable. And Cheez Whiz is *not* dairy. I checked. Also, according to so-called "nutritionists," getting your child to chew a gummy bear vitamin every morning does not right all the nutritional wrongs you've just committed. Whatever.)

Both media and sociologists have conditioned us to try to strive for an ideal family dinner. They never tire of telling us about the studies; you know, the ones that show the more often children bond with you over a family dinner, the more likely they are not to get into drugs or teenage sex, or to flunk out of school. I believe that's asking an awful lot of a meatloaf, but bear with me as I ponder this ideal. Picture the kids happily chatting away about their school escapades, your husband beaming at you from the end of the table, you proudly serving up a wholesome meal that you've effortlessly and lovingly prepared. Yeah, um, not so much. And dinner is just *one* of the meals most moms are expected to produce and orchestrate with relative ease—all while savouring the joy and happiness that can only come from spending quality time with their families. Okey dokey.

In my house, there are four kids between the ages of seven and 17, each with his or her own particular and annoying eating peccadilloes ("the plastic plate with the fish on it makes the food taste better!"). Add in an assortment of schools, sport lessons and practices to get to, and a distracted and overworked husband. Top it all off with me—the reluctant cheerleader and cook whose overriding thought during every meal is not of harmonious family order, but more of "I don't really care if you hate it. Just shut up and frigging eat it. I got things to do." (Did you notice there wasn't an ounce of sentiment about family bonding time in there? Darn.) So, you get the picture, right? No ideals here; just plain old reality.

My favourite writer, satirist Dorothy Parker, used to mutter the immortal words "What fresh hell is this?" every time her doorbell rang or her telephone jingled. (Yes, in her day, a telephone did truly jingle, not beep, buzz, or play "Boom Boom Pow.") Dorothy didn't have children—I do believe she would have drowned them within days, so it's just as well—but I still draw on her reflective response for my own world. From the cries of "Did you make something good for a change?" to "There's a vein in my chicken!", the start of any process that involves getting food into my children signals the start of my own fresh hell . . . every day. At least *two or three times* a day. It shouldn't be surprising to me anymore (but it still is) that more often than not, my darling family—or, as they see themselves around the kitchen table, "the unfortunately incarcerated"—are just not happy with the bland prison fare I've managed to serve up. And I am definitely *not* their happy matron.

However, in the face of this adversity I have somehow managed to compile some easy to make, foolproof recipes that would likely *never* grace the pages of the culinary-porn cookbooks that overflow on bookstore shelves, or be featured on energetic and eclectic television cooking shows, and yet they do (mostly) put a (mostly) nutritious and (mostly) edible meal on the table for my (mostly) ungrateful family. And if you can get food on the table that won't kill them, you might even manage to sneak in a few family bonding moments. Granted, most will end with a sister getting smacked, but we take what we can get at our house. I suggest you do the same.

The Mother of Invention

I'm not a born cook. I'm not a born domestic anything. And why should I be? Because I have ovaries? I don't think so. But necessity is the mother of invention, and I'm the mother inventing this book in order to get the stupid breakfast/lunch/dinner on the table so we can all get on with the rest of our lives. When I told people my next book would be called *Shut Up and Eat*, the response was either a laugh or a sigh. All moms can relate this topic to their own child's life, from day one ("he won't latch on!") to young adulthood ("close the refrigerator door—dinner is in five minutes!"). For their entire stay on the planet, it seems, we mothers struggle to get our children to really, really, just shut up and eat.

Almost every mom I know goes through a daily battle with her children (and sometimes with her husband). It starts at about four o'clock, when the kids arrive home from school, or maybe a few hours later, when everyone shows up post-work and/or after-school activities. It continues until the end of the evening meal, and sometimes into the evening itself. In my house, that battle starts off sort of like this.

Offspring: "Mom, what's for dinner?"
Me: "Haven't thought about it." (Actually, I have thought about it, but I was instantly distracted by something shiny.)
Offspring: "Will it be something good?"
Me: "Doubt it. Hope you ate all of your lunch."

If, like me, you get distracted while cooking—was that a half open bottle of chardonnay in the fridge? Is that *Viva Las Vegas* on the movie channel? Nicholas, stop poking your sister with a wet sponge!—most of the recipes you need must have the ability to be started now, dabbled with later, and served up anytime. Now, with this book, you might even want to stop stirring, put up your feet, and read about some of my own culinary adventures. I'm sure you'll be able to relate. We'll get to the three square meals you're supposed to put on the table each day. We'll cover snacks, and, counterintuitively, dieting. We'll cover family dinners (or, as I call them, extreme eating events), and we'll even delve into the wild and wacky world of grocery shopping. Not a cold, hard biscuit unturned, I tell you. Along the way, I'll share some recipes that work for me and might work for you, too.

Before we get started, let me leave you with this comforting thought: It's not just the kids! Husbands, relatives, friends, acquaintances, other soccer moms, lunch supervisors, restaurant staff, grocery store clerks, ice cream truck drivers; all of these and more have the ability to drive me stark raving mad over food-related issues. From the snack spreadsheet that now appears at every organized sport, to the "appropriate" treat to take to the end-of-year school party, food and feeding has become a minefield—just like everything else in this overexamined and overparented world. The bright side? The whole topic has provided me with some great material. I hope it will help you to stop cursing and start laughing, at least for a few minutes.

Now shut up. And read.

Kathy's Kitchen Definitions

Carlinary arts: Preparation and distribution of food that can be eaten in a car, with one hand.

Dessert-worthy: A meal that's worth stuffing down, no matter how nasty, in order to get to a surprisingly excellent dessert (i.e., One I didn't prepare myself).

Friday night: Universally accepted exemption from having to put something homemade or healthy on the table (religious circumstances notwithstanding).

Hot sauce: Miracle sauce that covers all complete cooking disasters. Also a handy diversionary tactic as children/guests frantically search for water.

Ketchup: Miracle sauce that covers all cooking sins.

Nasty: Almost everything I put in front of my vegan-wannabe daughter.

Personal space: What all children require around the dinner table in order to not kick, punch, pinch, poke, or puncture (on purpose) the person sitting next to them.

Precooked bacon: Manna from heaven.

Kathy's Rules of the Kitchen

1. A little mould never hurt anyone. Cut the corner off that cheese, scoop that green stuff out of the sour cream, and go for it.

2. Unlike their fresh counterparts, frozen, green vegetables never get soggy and multi-coloured (while they're still frozen, that is). Embrace them.

3. The correct answer to "What's for dinner?" is, "Something nasty that you will no doubt hate. I'll call you when it's ready." No reason at all to raise their hopes. If they can choke it down, we all win.

4. Use dessert as a bribe. All good things in life are bribes that help get something nasty accomplished. Get over yourself, Supermom.

5. If you use a cereal bowl and the dishwasher is not full of clean dishes, put the damn bowl in the dishwasher. When milk and Cheerios are combined and sit for more than an hour, they form an unbreakable bond with the bowl.

6. If food falls on the floor and you're still planning on cooking it some more, it's good to go. Just put it on someone else's plate.

7. Yes, children, all meat comes from one animal or another. Most of them are not very cute anyway, and live such short, miserable lives that they are never named nor do they experience any joy whatsoever. Let's move on, shall we?

8. When adding items to the grocery list, do not scribble "Something good." You'll get smacked once I figure out whose handwriting it is.

9. I do *not* get to make "Mommy's favourite" dish every single night of the week. First of all, that's not logistically possible. You can't have *seven* favourites, you frigging math geniuses. Second, if they were my favourites they would never include green beans or ketchup. This is for you, one way or the other.

10. I know all the hiding places for the peas and lima beans. Stop it.

11. Pasta out of a can is still pasta. Stop listening to Grandma. I ate my share of tinned spaghetti when I was a kid, trust me.

12. Beans on toast *is* a meal. Don't listen to your Uncle Kevin. Remember he's related to your Dad.. 'Nuff said.

13. Speaking of Dad: Barbecuing something for ten minutes means nothing around here. Just know that and set the table. *That* would be impressive.

14. You know that 30-second rule? I don't understand it. Chances are, you dropped it there in the first place, and I've never seen anyone in this house move that quickly to pick up something they've dropped. Let's go with three days, okay?

15. Don't eat a whole bag of cookies at once.

16. Do I really have to talk about the straight-from-the-carton drinking? Okay, okay. I'll stop.

Part 1
Family Meals

"The most remarkable thing about my mother is that for thirty years she served the family nothing but leftovers. The original meal has never been found."
—Calvin Trillin

1
Feeding Your Family
Moms and Dads and Food, Oh My!

"Save all culinary criticism until after you eat. Who knows, you might be so full that you forget what you were going to say."
—Alice's Unspoken Rules, *Alice's Brady Bunch Cookbook*, 1994

"I'm talking to you, Dad."
—Kathy Buckworth, *Shut Up and Eat*, 2010

We need to face facts. The family meal is fraught with disaster. It's a prescription written to fail, almost every time. You (the earnest mom) hate making the family meal day after day after day, and they (the annoying children) hate eating it. Mostly because *you* made it with your *own* hands, in your *own* kitchen, with disdainfully fresh and nutritious grocery-store ingredients. Come on, Mom! Everyone knows food goes through an amazing taste transformation once it's been passed through a drive-thru window. In fact, I'm thinking of installing one on the side of my house so the kids can grab their breakfast sandwiches as they ride by on their bikes. To make it really authentic, I'm thinking of charging them *and* getting the order wrong half the time. Hopefully I won't develop the prerequisite zits and an "uptalk" pattern of speech. And I'm nixing the hairnet, okay?

I honestly don't understand (or care, frankly) why my family doesn't love my cooking, or at least like it. But the whys don't really matter. The indisputable fact is that whether they (or we) like it or not, moms are "supposed" to get three meals down the adorable, little throats of our offspring by the end of each day. I'm pretty sure that rule is right upfront in every parenting book ever written. Whether we're serving these meals at home, or bundling them up and sending them out to schools and camps, the food is "supposed" to be healthy and lovingly prepared.

After 17 years of trying to achieve this balance, my advice is this: Go for one or the other. Either it's healthy or you loved making it. It can't really be both. (If it's neither, it's takeout.) If you knock yourself out making that perfectly nutritious meal each and every time, I have to tell you, the love will surely be missing. If you're able to snatch a Lunchable out of the fridge, throw in an apple and a Wagon Wheel cookie, and send them on their way in five seconds or less, you're going to feel the love. Maybe not for the kids, but for the packaged-goods company that just helped you out. It's all good from where I'm standing, baby.

And on and on it goes—from breakfast, to lunch, to dinner. And don't forget the inevitable snacks. Oh yes, the snacks. Honestly, when did we become a society in which children are not expected to go more than 16 seconds without being fed a "snack"? When did we start adhering to some unwritten law that states our children may never be hungry or uncomfortable in any way? Oh, yes. Since we all decided to be obese, that's when. Never mind.

In the Beginning

Our epic struggle with food starts early. From the time we begin breast or bottle feeding, there's a battle to get just the right food into our wee ones' systems. In fact, that's the first battle, isn't it? Breast or bottle? There are good reasons for either choice, but rest assured that whichever path you choose you're going to hit some controversy. For the record, all four of mine were bottle-fed. (I really should provide self-addressed stamped envelopes with this book so you can start writing now. I've heard it all, save your energy.) Does that make me a bad mother? You know what? I don't care. My children are all healthy today, and to the best of my sleep-deprived recollection I didn't abandon them in a corn-field when they were infants so I have to conclude that the whole situation worked for me. And that's my main message. In a world full of "right" or "expert" ways, we seem to have lost "our" way.

I remember a visit to a dim sum restaurant with a friend when my son Nic was about two years old. As Nic was my fourth child, I knew that a busy dim sum experience could keep a toddler busy and entertained. I also knew that it was entirely possible that he wouldn't eat a bite of the wondrous array of food in front of us. So I did what moms have been doing for generations—I brought a box of Smarties with me. Turns out I did this much to the disgust of the "good" parents at the next table, who were clearly sitting with prodigal child #1. Their stroller was clean (and in the restaurant with them), and they had a stockpile of toys, wipes, books, and an arsenal of plastic-lidded containers offering a plethora of prewashed, precut, and, I believe, colour-coordinated healthy foods for their child to eat. They tsk-tsked over my Smartie doling while they smugly attempted to feed their child from their own bring-along smorgasbord. Much to my delight and pathetic need for self-validation, their child was having none of this. He kept spying the brightly coloured candy disks my child was stuffing down his throat—and occasionally, accidentally, throwing on the floor. At the end of their meal, the lovely couple decided to allow their angel genius child to display his cuteness and startling mobility (so gifted!) and let him walk around the restaurant. He did this, stopping only to pick up the dirty Smarties my son had thoughtfully left for him on the floor. Then he ate them. *Ba ha ha ha ha ha!* Who's the expert now?

So the kids have it figured out. And the seasoned mom—at least the one not brainwashed or peer-pressured into Supermom tendencies—knows how to get her child through a meal. Note the wording there: *Through* a meal—both in terms of time and nutrition. Sometimes these are mutually exclusive (see above restaurant example). Most of the Moms I know figure this out at about the same time as one of their children is enrolled in an organized sport, which naturally trumps familial bonding and nutrition.

Several (Choice) Words about Dad

So moms can get it right—and get it done—by trusting their instincts. But what about dads? Rumours abound regarding New Age Dads who are supposed to be picking up 50% of the domestic duties, a huge portion of which includes feeding the family. Well, maybe I'm unique, but at my house, getting Dad involved in the family feeding process is an uphill battle.

For example, I give him a shopping list for the grocery store. (Wait. First, I need to direct him there ... you know, honey, it's the big building with the shopping carts outside that *isn't* The Home Depot). Okay. Back to the list. I have prepared this because the thought of him knowing the precise moment we're out of broccoli or toilet paper is just ridiculous. And yes, the realization that I *do* know this does sadden me. But I digress. List in hand, hubby will proceed to the store to do the most annoying thing ever. He will "shop the list." What I mean by this is that he doesn't add a single item to the cart that isn't on the list. This is in complete contradiction to the way men shop at the aforementioned Home Depot, where every shiny he-man article on the shelf miraculously leaps into his hands. At the grocery store, however, when he sees juice boxes on sale for a ridiculously low price, it doesn't occur to him that with four kids we might actually go through these a skid-load at a time, and that perhaps he should purchase some. Why? Because he has *no clue* what a juice box costs regularly, and *no idea* where or how they are used. They just magically appear in the soccer bag, lunch bag, and picnic area. Hell, I consider myself lucky if he remembers that we have four children.

So, he arrives home from the store, drops the groceries on the kitchen table and says "There." There frigging what? Like you've done me some huge favour? Put them away, you big goof. No! Not there. Oh, seriously—I'll just do it myself. Go play with a saw or something.

If men are interested at all in cooking the food you actually have in your cupboard, they will first assess its barbecue-ibility. Because everyone knows that standing in front of an open gas flame is manly. If the food in question can be BBQ'd, the men are in. If it can't—well, it had better involve a can opener. My husband's signature dish is Corned Beef Hash. Corned beef from a can, frozen hash browns from the freezer, and a hacked up onion. Of course it's good—that's not the point. And yes, you're right, sweetie, I should have put hash browns on the list. How else could you possibly have known that we needed them? You don't have the intra-uterine grocery signal device, like I do.

But wait a minute. Perhaps I'm being a tad unfair. I do understand that there are men out there who are good cooks. Sure, it's normally on a Saturday night with a beer and a BBQ or a glass of red and a pasta recipe, but does it really matter? As long as I'm not cooking, who cares? Still, it seems to me that the ones who can *really* cook—the *great* ones—leap straight from the backyard into running the kitchen of one of the most expensive restaurants in town, likely with their own reality-TV cooking show, in which they yell. A lot. Not a lot of these guys turn up in "Family Meal Land: Open Daily." More's the pity.

Given this sorry state of affairs, I've basically concluded that it's mostly the moms who are out there tracking down the latest chicken recipe, even when they know there hasn't been a new one invented since 1957. It's moms who are worrying about the amount of healthy food their children are eating. And it's moms making sure that if their offspring have to eat in public, the proper tools and strategies are in place. Dads, nice try on the nutrition thing. Thanks for coming out.

Oh, hell. I can't help it. I need to share another story from my personal arsenal about the whole dad-food conundrum. While I was on a book tour for *The BlackBerry Diaries*, my husband took all four kids to his family's vacation home in Northern Quebec. I knew there was a BBQ, and his mother was just down the street, so I had high hopes that the kids would eat a few decent meals. Except when he was on his own. For some unknown reason, he picked just such a night to call me. The conversation went something like this:

Him: Hey, the kids wanted to talk to you.
Me: Great! Put them on.
17-year-old daughter: What?
Me: What are you doing?
17: Just sitting down to dinner.
Me: (silently thinking, then why did he just call me?) What are you having?
17: Canned pasta.
Me: Honestly, you call that dinner?
17: I call it *heaven*, Mom. And you never make it.
Me: Put someone else on.
10-year-old daughter: Hey, Mom. Can't talk. Dad's yelling at us to eat dinner.
Me: (to a dial tone) Bye.

That was as satisfying as the meal they were just about to eat.

Kids in the Kitchen. A Recipe for Disaster

It doesn't happen often, but once in a while, my kids do express an interest in helping out in the kitchen. I'm not really a control freak, but watching those grubby little hands mix up and mangle cookie dough doesn't leave me craving the resulting baked goods. I suppose I should thank them for helping me out on my diet. They also have a few other helpful ways to reduce my caloric intake:

- Sticking their fingers directly into the three-cheese tortilla dip, just after I've spied that same digit firmly implanted in an unsavoury orifice.
- Taking a big swig of my soft drink and leaving one-third of a cheesie behind.
- Knocking over my wine during an unusually enthusiastic game of "throw the wiener."
- Poking my stomach and asking, "Well, if you're not pregnant, what's in there?"

And so there you have it—the unholy trinity of folk responsible for food-related issues in any given home: Mom, Dad, and Offspring. You'll notice that I've totally avoided the discussion of households in which an in-law or grandparent might be involved. That's a whole other ball of wax, and probably a topic worthy of its own book. Anyway, you can see, surely, how the problems start. So now that we know the key players—for better or for worse—we can move on to the meals themselves. Let the games begin.

2
Breakfast
The Most Annoying Meal of the Day

"Breakfast is the most informal of all family meals and because it is the first meal of the day it should be cheery as well as wholesome. So use colourful dishes and gleaming silver flatware against a gay tablecloth or mats to give the table maximum cheeriness."
—from *Glamour and the Hostess*, by Marie Holmes, Director, Chatelaine Institute, 1955

"Breakfast is a meal you have to stuff down your kids' throats before the bus comes and you can't find that damn mitten or permission form. Anything frozen, toaster-worthy, and with a hint of fruit will do. Use gleaming icing and a loud voice to give the eaters maximum incentive to grab and eat on the way out the door."
—from *Shut Up and Eat*, by Kathy Buckworth, Director, Getout-ofmyhouse Institute, 2010

Yes, yes, we know breakfast is supposed to be the most important meal of the day. Yes, yes, it helps your kids to use their brains more effectively at school, and for adults it's supposed to assist in sticking to a calorie-appropriate diet for the rest of the day.

It's also normally a yell-fest, at least if you have children in the house. Sadly, they haven't read the same research as you, and they're more interested in why you insist on sticking your big, fat head in the way of SpongeBob while you blather on about "time ticking," etc.

Here's how breakfast works at my house. It generally starts out the same way each day. After the kids drag their butts out of bed (it's not a weekend, so they don't feel compelled to get up at 6:30 a.m.), they stagger down into the family room and sit, zombie-like, in front of either a cartoon or a game that involves "getting kills." Once I place myself directly in the line of the screen, and they grow tired of trying to see around me, I am able to make eye contact. At this point, I try to ascertain exactly what it is they would like to eat prior to going to school. Often, I am met with this response.

Kid: Well, what do we have?

Me: ("in my head" voice) Same crap we always have, Einstein. What, do you think you woke up in an IHOP by mistake? ("out loud" voice) You know what we have. Cereal, toast, frozen things with icing, waffles, fruit.

Kid: (Silence.)

Me: Helloooo. Tell me what you want or you won't get any breakfast.

Kid: What? I told you.

Me: (in head) Crap. Was I looking at my BlackBerry? (out loud)
  Um, sure. You said you wanted cereal, right?"
Kid: NO! You never buy any good cereal! You always get what
  HE likes!(Emphasizes point by hurling the TV remote at a
  stunned younger brother.)
Brother: What was that for? I'm going to punch you.
Me: (in head) How much money do I have saved up? (out loud)
  Okay, you little boogers, *I'm* picking your breakfast and
  you're eating it. Now go and get dressed!
Both kids: "You're so mean! We hate you! And we're not going
  to school!"
Me: Sigh.

Usually, eventually, I'm able to get each child to choose
something to eat, and I will admit to allowing them to eat their
breakfasts in the family room, in front of the TV. This way, I can
work on my laptop in the kitchen and supervise what's being
taken out of the cupboards by the teenagers. Always thinking,
that's me.

This loose breakfast strategy generally works well, although
it does have its flaws. The other day, my 7-year-old said to me, "I
can't finish my soft-boiled egg because I got my toe stuck in it."
Now, to many a childless person, that might sound a little weird,
but around here, it's par for the course. The good news? He was
actually attempting to eat something that fell into the "breakfast
food" category, and it was *his* toe that the egg was stuck on—
not the body part of an unsuspecting sibling, or, let's face it, his
own penis.

By way of explanation, let me just say that the coffee table
where I placed his egg-and-toast plate is low. Also, the poor

bugger is a male and hence unable to focus on both eating and watching at the same time. (Have you *seen* guys try to eat and watch the Super Bowl? It's not pretty.) For a 7-year-old, trying to simultaneously dip toast soldiers and watch *Power Rangers* is a similar enterprise. Toe or no toe, he was eating, and I'll take my victories where I can find them, thank you very much.

Dinner for Breakfast and Other Adventures

Breakfast at my house is all about compromise. For example, I've long since gotten over the idea that "breakfast food" has to, in fact, fit some preordained notion of what "breakfast food" actually is. Oatmeal is great (apparently, although I can't stand the stuff), but who said hot cereal was the end all and be all? Ditto with pancakes. Sure, they're nice and fluffy and fit easily into a food group, but is that all? And what about this concept of whole grains and fruit? A healthy start, absolutely, but be prepared to find yourself watching the school bus leave without your children on board, while Healthy Johnny is still dawdling over his vanilla yogurt, bran buds, and freshly sliced strawberries. His nutrition for your blood pressure level? I don't think so.

When children and breakfast are combined, I find that creative thinking works best. Grilled cheese and bacon? Alright. Leftover canned pasta? I suppose. I *do* draw the line at cooking up unopened junk foods (i.e., get your hands off that new box of mac and cheese), but if a certain food is acceptable for us to serve at lunch or dinner, why not breakfast?

In an effort to counterbalance anything that might be upsetting to the nutritional universe during the day, I've also taken to serving "breakfast for dinner." My kids *love* bacon and eggs for dinner (except the vegan wannabe, but that's another boring story), and French toast is often a hit as well. The moral of the story? If you turn your breakfast thinking a tiny bit on its side, you'll discover that you can get through the half-hour of hell before the bus comes and send them off with full stomachs. Look, they're out of your house and that's the most important part, right?

Weekend Rules

Weekend breakfasts are a whole other beast. If my house is typical (and I really hope it isn't, for the sake of everyone else), Dad tends to take on the responsibility of Saturday morning breakfast. Perhaps the risk of being hit by a stray piece of bacon fat is akin to the inherent danger of having the barbecue blow up. Not sure. At any rate, while it's terrific that Dad takes charge of at least one meal a week, I nevertheless have some basic rules I'd like to pass along.

1. Try to keep track of which children you fed, at what time, how much, and why. This information is important for when we get to the hockey/karate/dance class part of the schedule and they are either too full or faint to participate. At that point, I will have wasted a car trip and I will not be happy. You want to avoid this situation. Trust me.

2. If you and the children finish off the cereal box, the appropriate storage place is not back in the cupboard, or on top of the counter. We have this new thing called "recycling." Read the pamphlet, doofus.

3. Put your own personal preferences aside and actually suggest to the children that they might like some fruit as a part of their breakfast. In fact, better yet, wash it, cut it up, and put it in front of them. Nine times out of ten they will eat it. For instructions on how to cut up a nectarine, ask the preschooler.

4. If you leave the margarine out on the counter one more time I will shove it someplace that the sun does not shine. It'll be in liquid form, so it won't hurt. Much.

5. Please stop putting leftover pieces of toast in a resealable bag and threatening to make the kids eat them later. You never do it and they know this. They win. And you've never once thrown out any type of leftover you put into the fridge. Plus, you've used up the last resealable bag and you never go to the grocery store to buy more. It's just annoying on so many levels.

6. It should take one bowl, one measuring cup, and one frying pan to make pancakes. Just sayin'.

Armed with these handy rules, most men make adequate breakfast chefs. Sometimes, they even get adventurous. My husband once asked me how to make a hard-boiled egg. He refused to believe what I told him and looked it up. I say, Fill yer boots, buddy! In fact, while you're at it, why don't you look up recipes for the next 817 family meals? That'll be the next six month's worth, FYI.

So what's the bottom line on this "most important" meal of the day? Keep it simple, stupid. Breakfast doesn't have to be hard, it just has to be food. Sometimes, the best opportunities for family bonding moments come when you thrust that granola bar into their hands as they run out the front door for the bus. Look, you didn't hit them and they didn't swear at you. If that isn't a joyous moment, I don't know what is. Now clean up those breakfast dishes and get ready to deal with the next circle of family-meal hell: lunch.

Breakfast Recipes

Okay, maybe "recipe" is a stretch when you're talking about breakfast at my house. Maybe "options-when-your-toaster-appropriate-foods-are-depleted descriptions" would be better.

Dippy Egg with Soldiers

I'm including this recipe to help out men who might be trying to figure out what to prepare when Mom has had major surgery or she has some other similar lame excuse for not getting up and making the family breakfast.

Ingredients
egg(s)
water
bread*

Directions
1. Place egg(s) in a sauce pan and cover with cold water.
2. Turn the element up to high and set your timer. Depending on the size of your saucepan, it will take between 9 and 12 minutes to soft boil an egg. The basic rule of thumb is that once the water is at a full boil, the eggs needs about one more minute.
3. Toast a piece (or pieces) of bread, and cut into 1/4-inch strips—these are the "soldiers."
4. Take the soft-boiled eggs out of the water with a spoon (using your hands is a little messy, what with the third-degree burns and all), and slice of the top of the egg, shell and all, with either a spoon or a knife. You can also do this the annoying way (i.e., the way most men do it) by cracking the egg and peeling the shell away and then digging your spoon into the soft flesh of the egg. This method must be accompanied by the words "ouch, ouch ouch," because (surprise!) the egg shell is hot. Doofus.

5. Serve egg and soldiers and tell the child(ren) to eat up so
    Mom can clean away the dishes before she has to leave for
    her post-op checkup. Try not to let anyone get their toe or
    other body part stuck in the food.

*Told you it was simple.

Breakfast Sandwich

"They have prewrapped sausages. Why don't they have prewrapped bacon?"
"Well, can you blame them?"
"Yeah!"

These immortal and prophetic words were uttered by the Barenaked Ladies in their hit song "If I Had a Million Dollars." And guess what, guys? They *do* have prewrapped bacon. It's pre*cooked* bacon, and it's *faaaabulous*! When it first came out, I thought to myself, "what kind of lazy slacker would buy that?" Turns out I would. And I love it. Perfect for breakfast sandwiches for the kids or a quick BLT for lunch. Here's one of my daughter's favourites before a hockey game (Note: can be eaten easily in a car).

Ingredients
English muffin
egg
2 slices fabulous precooked bacon
1 cheese slice (the faker the better)
mayonnaise, to taste

Directions
1. Toast the English muffin.
2. Heat up the precooked bacon in the microwave according to package directions (usually 10 seconds or less—faaabulous).
3. Crack the egg into a small frying pan and stir (but don't scramble) the yolk and white together. Cook until done.

4. Slide the egg onto the bottom half of the English muffin, top with bacon, cheese slice, and remaining English muffin half.

5. Slide sandwich into the microwave for 10 seconds to melt the cheese. (An alternate way of doing this is to skip the cheese and put on about 1/2 cup of mayonnaise—at least I think that's how much my daughter Bridget the Sauce Queen puts on.)

6. Get in the car and eat!

7. Get out your BlackBerry and catch up on email during the game. What? You didn't read my last book*?

*The BlackBerry Diaries: Adventures in Modern Motherhood is available wherever fine books are sold.

Banana Chocolate Chip Bread

Raise your hand if you have bananas in your house that are decidedly more black than yellow or green. If you're like me, this lovely, nutritious fruit seems to skip from green to black overnight. Relax! If you have four of these brown or black beauties around, you have the basic ingredient for a banana bread that can serve many purposes if you follow the directions carefully (and if you make it slightly wrong, it can be a terrific doorstop). Actually, the directions don't have to be followed that carefully—this my 10-year-old daughter Bridget's favourite recipe to make.

Ingredients
2 cups all-purpose flour
1 tsp baking soda
1/4 tsp salt
1/2 cup butter
3/4 cup brown sugar
2 eggs, beaten
2 1/3 cups mashed overripe bananas (about four)
1 cup (at least) chocolate chips

Directions
1. Preheat oven to 350°F. Lightly grease a 9 × 5 loaf pan.
2. Combine flour, baking soda, and salt. If you are doing this on a countertop that has your laptop within a 2-inch striking distance, remove the laptop. Trust me on this.
3. In a separate bowl, cream together butter and brown sugar.

Stir in eggs and mashed bananas until well blended. Stir the banana mixture into the flour mixture, just to moisten.

4. Pour batter into the loaf pan and bake for 65 minutes, until a toothpick inserted in the middle comes clean. Let bread cool in pan for 10 minutes, then turn out onto a wire rack. Stand guard by the bread with a metal spatula. Teens have noses, you know.

3
Lunches
Midday Disasters

*"Lunch for the family is usually a simple meal with **two** or **three** courses but the table should be attractively and neatly set."*
—Marie Holmes, Director, Chatelaine Institute, *Glamour and the Hostess*, late 1950s

"Lunch for the family is normally a simple sandwich with two to three ingredients (ketchup and / or mustard counting as one). The children are encouraged to eat between rounds of Call of Duty *and* Halo 3.*"*
—Kathy Buckworth (what, are you for real, Marie? You're starting to get on my nerves)

While weekends do sometimes provide the opportunity for a family lunch, weekdays are an entirely different story. I don't think we're alone in being a family who mostly has their lunches

apart—at a safe distance from annoying siblings and spouses—
during the week. Popular locations for the midday meal include
the office, a restaurant, or the dreaded school lunchroom or "caf-
egymatorium" featured at most high schools.

Now we all know the benefits of mac and cheese (none of
them nutritious, silly), so just buy the box and follow the directions. Yes, the colour of the cheese is an orange not found in nature, and, yes, it tastes like crap, but kids and men adore it. Go
figure. And it costs about 99 cents a box, so what's not to love?
Likewise canned pasta. I have actually convinced my children
that Chef Boyardee personally made this stuff so that it doesn't
require heating up, and tastes better out of the can. I still remember those old commercials with the dirty-looking kids running through the cobblestone streets of Italy, reacting to their
mother's calls for lunch. She was serving up what every authentic Italian mother would serve: canned pasta. Hey, if it was good
enough for them, it's good enough for me.

On the Road Again

I know many moms look forward to their kids being on summer vacation so they don't have to make school lunches. I don't
like to judge (ha!), but I think these women are insane.

What, kids don't eat lunch in the summer? Isn't it inherently
easier to make *all* the lunches in the morning (or the night before), instead of chasing the kids around the house for an hour
asking what they want to eat? Then, when you don't have what
they want, you have to listen to them complain about how
you're making whatever you're making, and watch them sneak

food from the snack cupboard while you're doing it?

I *love* giving my kids food that they'll be eating somewhere else. This way, I don't have to listen to the litany of complaints I regularly get during the "face-time" of breakfast and dinner. I make it and put it into their lunch bags. Once they flip open that soggy bag at their desks, their options are limited:

1. Eat it all and tell the other kids how their Mom is the best. *Hahahahahaha!*
2. Eat only the good bits (cookies, chips, etc.) and toss the fruit and sandwiches.
3. Trade away all the fruit and sandwiches for some hapless kid's cookies and chips.
4. Don't eat it and suck it up. The lunch supervisor doesn't care that you don't like the crusts or the angle of the knife cut on your ham sandwich.
5. Whine to the kid beside you about how much you the hate your lunch, only to have them respond with, "Have you ever tried licking a cat?"

I recently went on a field trip where we had to bring both our own and our children's lunches. When my 7-year-old son and I sat down to eat lunch, I was amazed at the diversity of the offerings. Spying both the most nutritious (i.e., brown and grainy looking) and the most expeditious (a half-eaten Krispy Kreme), it would appear to me that most moms are still struggling with the appropriate packed lunch inventory. My son had his regular white-bread-and-jam sandwich, with some cookies, a pear, and a small chocolate. Yawn. He ate half the sandwich, two bites of the pear, and the chocolate. Then he threw the rest out. Since I wasn't going to have to listen to his "I'm so hungry" whining in the afternoon when he was back in class, I let him do it. But I didn't really need to know he did that with his lunch. Somehow, I had myself convinced that his behaviour at home (he'd never willingly take fruit, eat a whole sandwich, or skip the chocolate option) was the anomaly. Once he was at school, I told myself, he would be downright exemplary in his eating habits. Do you see what I'm saying about the lunch angle, ladies? Out of sight, out of mind. Delusions intact.

My LOSE-THE-LUNCH Campaign

In a world of over-snacked children, lunch has become just another pit stop. When I was a kid, lunch was the first thing you ate after your Count Chocula, which had been consumed many hours before. Today, kids are not only allowed but also encouraged to take snacks out with them at morning recess. So school lunches have to include an easily dispensable snack as well as a non-peanut-bearing sandwich. This can be tough.

At home, the snack culture continues. On the weekends, my kids routinely graze the cupboards mid-morning. Not surprisingly, when lunchtime arrives, and I attempt to feed them a tuna salad sandwich or a contraband peanut butter and jam, they announce that they're not hungry—until an hour later when they're grazing the cupboards again. Sigh. At this point, I'd like to start a "Lose the Lunch" campaign. In fact, there's so little to say about lunches that this chapter is over. I gotta go find a sandwich.

Oh, wait, this chapter is not quite over. Just saying the word "sandwich," which in my mind defines lunch, reminds of the time we took our kids up north to visit some friends at their cottage. The wife was a notoriously picky eater (yep, the same one who brings her own food to my house for a dinner party—wonder how she's doing these days) who refused to eat anything that didn't come from a speciality market or a mysterious-looking store in a trendy part of town, or that hadn't recently been written up in *Pretentious Foodie* magazine. (Okay, no that magazine doesn't really exist, but it should. I know many people who would unabashedly subscribe to it.) I offered to bring up a meal, thinking that at least we could feed all the kids, and ourselves, something that didn't resemble poo on a 10-grain cracker.

So, what's lunch to me? To me, lunch—especially when you have to feed five children under the age of 12—is a bunch of buns (some can even be whole wheat, if you insist), some sliced ham, salami, and roast beef, mustard and mayonnaise, and cheese, lettuce, and tomatoes, and you're ready to go.

Or so I thought. As I unloaded our food contribution to the cottage weekend, I could see our hostess's face wrinkle up in disgust. I could tell she was picturing my shopping expedition at a common, well-lit, fairly priced neighbourhood big-box supermarket. "Oh, you can just put your luncheon meat in the fridge and we can have that if we get desperate," she sniffed. "Or if your children don't like what I've brought for lunch. It's a customary Egyptian meal that will take about an hour to prepare. It may be too sophisticated for their palates. Or yours. In which case there's always the luncheon meat."

You mean, in which case there's always the four friggin' bottles of wine I brought, you sanctimonious little—oh, whatever. Half of me was determined to enjoy the mid-eastern delight she was about to bestow on my unsuspecting family (whose mouths were already watering at the thought of a towering ham and mayo sub). The other half of me was ready to tell her to knock her skinny little socks off and have her complicated lunch while we chowed down on the porch, car keys at the ready.

Predictably, the lunch was bland. It was full of some sort of pasty yellow pea mixture, and my kids hated it. Because of their unsophisticated palates, of course. That and the fact that it tasted like dog food.

And *that*, my friends, is the end of the lunch chapter. And in case you were wondering—yes, I'm okay with not getting invited back to that particular cottage.

Lunch Recipes

Okay, you get the picture for lunch around my place. Either it's being prepackaged for consumption somewhere else or it's being thrown on the table in between sports practices. Figuring that you're in the same boat (you bought the book, didn't you?), I'll share some of my tried-and-true concoctions.

Peanut Butter and Jam Sandwich

Children who have grown up in the "peanut-free school" world (which began, to the best of my recollection, in about 1995) might never have experienced the beauty of this classic sandwich. Here it is, with a few suggestions for variations.

Ingredients
peanut butter (smooth is for wimps, crunchy is for the hearty)
jam (any type will do, but classic is strawberry)
white bread (come on, go all the way with this one—go Wonderbread!)

Directions
1. Spread the peanut butter all over the bread in big swirls, just like they do on television. Go big or go home.
2. Spoon the jam onto the other side of the bread.
3. Slam the two pieces of bread together with lightning speed.
4. Don't cut it. Eat it whole. Perfect.

My kids like to replace the jam with Nutella, or banana, or cucumber, or even ketchup. You're hitting a few food groups in there, so go for it. After all, you've got to finish that jar of peanut butter before you have other people's children over again.

Classic Grilled Cheese

Another favourite in my house is the grilled cheese sandwich. I remember eating these beauties every Sunday, after church, at the athletic club my family used to belong to. Before we could strap on ice skates, jump in the pool, play badminton, or go bowling (was there really a time when I did four sports in one day, just for the fun of it?), we would hit the cafeteria and get a grilled cheese sandwich with a pickle. None of us actually liked the pickles, but we always asked for it because if you placed it on a square napkin, grabbed both ends of the napkin and quickly pulled it tight, you could launch that pickle on to the ceiling of the cafeteria, where it would stay for months. Ah, good times.

Ingredients

1 or 2 slices of processed cheese (I prefer Kraft)
2 slices of white bread (again, yes, I know, I know)
margarine
optional extras: bacon, tomato, ham

Directions

1. Turn the stove element to medium heat, and warm up a small non-stick frying pan.
2. Spread the margarine evenly on two pieces of bread.
3. Put one piece of bread margarine-side down in the pan.
4. Place the cheese on top, adding the optional extras, if desired.
5. Place the last piece of bread on top, margarine-side up.
6. Flip after a couple of minutes. Keep flipping until both sides of the bread are light brown.

7. Cut into triangles. This is key. The sandwich will not taste the same otherwise.

8. Serve with a pickle if desired, but no napkin.

The Weekend Picnic Lunch

Every few years, we travel to my husband's family summer vacation spot, a quaint little village called Tadoussac, about three hours north of Quebec City. The total drive from our home is about 13 hours, which seems like 13 days when travelling with four children. Normally, by the time we get there I am truly in a vacation mode. I'd like to take a vacation from preparing food altogether, but my husband seems to balk at eating poutine for every single meal (although my 10-year-old daughter would gladly join me on this crusade). Luckily, lunches are normally a picnic affair, and we've managed to get the preparation down to an art. We stop at the small village grocery store, load up an insulated knapsack and hit the trail to one rocky beach or another where my children are sure to pick up scrapes, bug bites, and the occasional garden snake. All good fun—if you've been doing it for 40 years. I haven't.

Anyway, here's my list of must-have's for any picnic lunch—no preparation required.

- 1 or 2 French loaves—4, if you happen to have my teenage son along with you for some reason.
- Paté—most kids (except my vegan-wannabe daughter) love paté. It's salty and sometimes garlicky and as long as you don't call it meat spread, they'll eat it.
- Cheese—some stinky for the grown-ups, some regular cheddar for the kiddies.
- Peanut butter—if you're allowed.
- Fruit—individual fruits that don't need cutting are best, like

plums, apples, nectarines, peaches, and grapes. Kids can pick these up and walk away. Emphasis here is on the walking away, because you also packed a little bottle of *wine*, didn't you? (In Quebec this is allowed—one of the key reasons I agree to go year after year.)

- Cookies or chips of some kind—you will go through the whole bag.
- Juice boxes for the kids, wine for the grown-ups—weren't you paying attention?

Make sure you take a spreading knife, a cutting knife, a cutting surface, and you're done. One last note: Just like the meals they serve at camp, picnic food tastes better if you're hungry (I recommend a good 10 km walk before settling for the picnic) and if it's the only thing in front of you. Plan accordingly.

4
Family Dinners
The Main Event

"There are a lot of people who must have the table laid in the usual fashion or they will not enjoy the dinner."
—Christopher Morely

"Those people are not invited to my house."—Kathy Buckworth

Is there anything more special and heart-warming than a good, old-fashioned family dinner? Well, let's see. Dropping a skateboard on your ankle or stapling your fingers together could come a close second, if your house is anything like my house.

Of course, we all have visions of what these special moments spent bonding over a home-cooked meal are going to be like. A freshly carved roast, steaming (and especially creamy) mashed potatoes, beaming faces, intelligent conversations. But here's the thing. We are idiots. Those visions will *never* come true, unless you're living on the set of *Little House on the Prairie* or *Leave it to Beaver*. (Even then, the Beav could be a little rascal at the table, and June never actually sat down with the family.) At my house there's fighting, whining, complaining, food throwing, and insult hurling. Once my husband and I call the kids to the table, it just gets worse.

During the week we're all exhausted from our busy days (in my case, that's any day that doesn't include a pedicure). Yet the media, both through television shows and commercials, has conditioned us to expect a heart-warming reunion over the daily dinner. In reality, it's more a coming together of a bunch of really bad attitudes.

Roses and Thorns

In order to pre-empt some of the fighting, and to keep the conversation light and flowing, my husband and I have instituted a little game we call "Roses and Thorns." In theory, each family member shares a "Rose" (or good thing) of the day, and a "Thorn" (bad thing). We immediately learned to enforce a rule prohibiting the daily Thorn from being "My brother is an idiot," or some similarly charming sentiment.

Here's an example of how that system is currently working for us.

Me: Who would like to start our Rose and Thorn tonight?
Nic: Me! I'm the youngest. I start. I get to start. Pick me pick me pick me pick me.
Me: Okay, it's you. Go.

Nic: *(Silence . . . followed by more silence.)*

Alex: God, you're such an idiot, Nic.

Nic: Mom! I get to go first! I know, my Rose is that we had school today.

Alex: You're really an idiot.

Bridget: How come you never ask me to go first? I have a good one today. You like Nic better!

Me: Bridget, sit down and eat and then you can go next.

Bridget: I can't sit down. I just went poo.

Alex: Well, there's my Thorn right there.

Nic: I wasn't finished! I still have a Thorn!

Victoria: My Rose is that I'm going away to university next year.

Alex: That's *everybody's* Rose, Vic.

Me: Alex! You go if you're such a smarty with these Roses and Thorns.

Alex: Yeah, right. Like that's going to happen. Can I go play basketball? I'm finished.

Nic: I haven't finished! My Thorn is I had a little accident.

Me: What? Where? And sit down, Bridget!

Bridget: I know where—I saw it in the bathroom. That was going to be my Thorn but I wasn't sure if I could say it because it's about Nic.

Alex: Bye, Mom *(door slam)*.

Victoria: Yeah, okay, whatever. I don't have to eat this, do I? Come on, Mom. Even you have to admit this chicken is gross.

Bridget: Anyway my Rose is—

Nic: It's still my turn!

Me: Pass the wine, Steve.

Steve: Does anyone want to know my Rose today?

Remaining family members, standing and sitting: NO!

As you can see, it's a bit of a work in progress. At best, it's a diversionary tactic designed to distract the family from the meal that's in front of them, which I know the majority of them won't like.

While we're on the subject of likes and dislikes, let me just say that finding recipes that the whole family will enjoy, all at the same time, is virtually impossible. I think that's more than okay. If you can sort of please some of the people some of the time (and ensure that you're always in the "some of the people" camp yourself), then you win.

Because, after all, you're also supposed to be spending this time engaged in quality family bonding (see my above discussion as an example), catching up on the day's events, and re-establishing the love and harmony only your special little unit has.

Yeah, whatever. Mostly you're trying to feed them, yell at them, check the calendar to see who has soccer, and where the dance competition is, figure out if you have enough gas to get there, and whether you can find an adequate "snack" for the entire team in your depleted cupboards, *and* not to freak out on the husband down the table, who is picking through his chicken looking for undercooked parts. (One time—a little food poisoning—and now you can't be trusted.) If you manage to have a conversation with your family at the dinner table that *doesn't* involve one of the following sentences, then I think you're doing pretty well:

- Should I call the teacher back this time?
- Yes, I can see the stain, and yes, it looks like poo. Change your clothes.

- Yes, *asshole* is a swear word.
- No, I didn't get your bristol board today. Perhaps you would like me to pull a piece out of my—oh, right, it's a swear word. Elbow.
- Gee, honey, no I didn't get the chance to pick up the garbage tags from the recreation centre 20 minutes away. Did you?
- Who's smelling your pee but you, anyway? Eat your asparagus.
- If I want to check my BlackBerry, I will. Maybe I'll call your teacher on it too. Yeah, thought that would shut you up.
- Okay *that* stain smells like poo, too.
- No, dear. I don't know if we have any beer. I don't drink beer. Haven't for a decade. Do you know if we have any tampons?

Most days, I am absolutely thrilled if we can get through dinner without an explosive bodily function, head slap, or conversation that ends with one of my daughters stomping away and slamming a door. The trick, I've discovered, is to get something on the table that at least some of the people will like, some of the time. If your schedule allows, judge the mood of the contestants before they sit down and pander to the one who will be the most trouble. I created this handy chart that I tape to my kitchen cupboard, for easy reference. Maybe it can help you.

CHILD	SITUATION	FOOD REMEDY
Nicholas, age 7	broken light sabre + pee incident at school =	BBQ Ribs
Bridget, age 10	fight with best friend over cutest Jonas brother + another day on this earth without a hamster =	Hamburgers
Alexander, age 15	cancelled Weezer concert + Mom spoke to his friends and tried to be funny =	Chicken Wings
Victoria, age 17	bad hair day (Mom's fault) + all clothes suddenly suck it =	Fettucine Alfredo

Oops—there, I just let a prime parenting secret out of the bag. Yes, we play favourites sometimes, and yes, we make life unfair for some of you more often than for others. Deal with it.

Sunday Dinner

One tradition we have managed to stick to (mostly) is the Sunday Family Dinner. Both my husband and I grew up in households where the big Sunday meal more often than not featured roast beef, Yorkshire puddings, potatoes, and gravy. This is a tradition we had been passing on to our kids.

A few years ago, though, I was asked to film a segment for a television show called *Yummy Mummy* hosted by '80s Much-Music VJ turned founder of the Yummy Mummy Club, Erica Ehm. Our segment was on finding activities to suit a family with such a wide variety of ages—at the time our children ranged from three to 14. It was hard to find things that the older kids and the younger wanted to participate in at the same time and, when we spoke to the Life Coach hired for the segment, he suggested we think about an activity that we were already doing as a family, and to build on it. My husband and I both blurted out "eating! We do Sunday dinner together." And the Life Coach said "Great! Why do the kids love it so much?" And we looked at each other and said, "They don't! They hate it!" Why? Well, further exploration revealed that Steve and I always picked the meal and we usually picked the same thing. So, post Life-Coach encounter, we adjusted our tradition. Now, every week we pick a name out of hat and that person gets to pick the family meal. I'll admit that some of the choices are a bit unorthodox (Fettuccine Alfredo and corn on the cob, or disgusting chili cheesedogs spring to mind), but with a little guidance, this has become a highlight of the kids' week. Well, maybe not a highlight for their whole week, but for our family mealtime at any rate.

One last word of advice. Do not—I repeat, do not—be afraid to use dessert as a bribe. It's a bribe. We know it's a bribe, and the kids know it's a bribe. Don't listen to all the nutritionists and parenting experts who tell you that promising children pudding only if they eat their carrots is setting them up to believe that sweet foods are a reward, and nutritious food a chore. They're right, but any doofus kid could figure this out, so I say go for it. Just like in other areas of life; you swallow the bad stuff and you get a reward at the end of the day. Dessert doesn't have to be anything more than a bag of store-bought cookies slammed on to the table—it's all you have time for anyway, because you have to get to that parent–teacher meeting, hockey game, volunteer event, whatever.

So there it is; Sunday dinner in a nutshell. It's not so scary, right? Regardless of how you and your brood sort it out, the family dinner *is* an important part of most families' lives. I'll admit I use it mostly for a head count and to set up the night's shower schedule, but that works for me. Find a reason to have one at your house and use it for your own purposes. It's worth it.

BBQ Me Up

Part of the reason barbecuing is so appealing is that it seems to throw away the constraints of the kitchen and let the outdoors rule. However, this freedom from the tyranny of mealtime can easily be taken to out-of-control levels without some basic rules. Lucky for you, I came across some of these rules in the 1961 version of Betty Crocker's *Outdoor Cook Book*. Let me share one with you now:

Develop some stern method of kibitzer control. People who would not dream of regulating your kitchen oven seem unable to resist "helping" the outdoor chef by stirring up his fire. They mean well. Indeed, such activity usually shows the first gleam of determination to try outdoor cooking for themselves. But threaten them off with the tongs, if necessary. Two firemasters is one too many.

I just *love* the idea of one suburban dad chasing another around his backyard with a pair of barbecue tongs, while Betty in her apron looks on approvingly. Handbags at noon, ladies. And is it just me, or do we not use the word *kibitzer* nearly enough when dealing with unruly children and adults?

Truly though, one of the great things about barbecuing is that it is normally relatively easy to suck the man of the house into actually cooking. Something to do with an open flame and the inherent explosive danger proves irresistible to these gullible fellows. Of course, the big downside is because they have spent a good 20 minutes searing a steak, they expect to get the credit for the entire meal, which, by the way, consists of salad, potatoes, fruit, and dessert, all of which has taken *you* about two hours to complete. It's okay, we can let them have this. The barbecuing gets them out of the kitchen, into the backyard, and out of our hair. Personally, I try to find additional things for my husband to do while in the backyard manning the grill—including garbage cleanup, putting the hose away, backwashing the pool, installing some fencing. . . . Be creative and see how far it takes you. It is important, however, to make sure that hubby isn't so distracted by these secondary activities that he forgets the meat on the barbecue itself. I learned this the hard way during an unfortunate oak-plank/flaming beef episode. Remember these are men; not universally known for their multi-tasking skill set.

Also, be prepared for the following conversation:

Him: Okay, honey, so I'll take care of dinner tonight. I picked up some steaks.
Me: Great. So what are we having with them?

Him: Potatoes and corn.

Me: You have that?

Him: We always have potatoes and corn in the house. (*Sadly, we do.*)

Me: Okay, whatever.

Him: Right then, I'm starting up the barbecue.

Me: Yeah, listen, I only need about an hour to get the other stuff ready. You might want to wait.

Him: (*Gone outside.*)

Me: *%^&*ng idiot.

Him: I'm ready for those steaks now.

Me: Fabulous. Hope they need about 40 minutes on the barbecue because that's how long the rest of the dinner is going to take. Hey, who's setting the table?

Him: (*Back outside again, stopping only to grab a beer out of the fridge.*)

Me; %^$&#*ng idiot. Kids, get in here and set the table and help me husk the corn!

Him: Okay, we're almost done.

Me: Stupendous. Just cut my finger with a knife while trying to peel the potatoes because *your* son used the potato peeler to whittle a stick last week. Oh, yeah. The corn is still hard and we've only found four forks.

Him: (*Gone. The sound of a beer cap twisting can be heard from the deck.*)

Me: ^&$^#ng idiot. Ouch. Crap. Damn.

Him: And we're ready. Kids, dinner!

Me: What the hell are you doing? The potatoes are half raw, the water for the corn hasn't boiled yet and I'm still on hold with Telehealth to see about this red line that's travelling up my arm from the cut on my finger.

Him: Mmmmmm. Now *that's* a steak. Your Dad knows how to cook, eh guys?

If you plan to go the barbecuing route during the week, you might want to make sure you have bagged salad, frozen French fries, or other "ready in an instant" side dishes in the fridge or freezer. As an alternative, you can also practise counting to ten. Whatever works for you.

Fondue Me

The appeal of a cauldron of hot boiling oil is perhaps an instinctual one for witchy women like me, but kids also like the sense of control that comes with cooking their own dinner right at the table. They get to pick what they like, cook it, dip it, and incinerate it—it's all good.

Once you have the children gathered around for the fantastic fondue experience, make sure that the flame is controllable and that you don't catch your youngest trying to burn little pieces of paper in it, or roast miniature marshmallows over it. Just sayin'.

If you're using an electric fondue pot, try to forget that what you're really doing is deep-frying perfectly nutritious pieces of food. Resist the urge to call each other Billy Bob or Lillie Mae. Also, don't refer to the meat as the "critter." Fondue is really just deep-frying with good P.R., just as a squirrel is a rat with good P.R. Sorry for just using "deep-fry" and "squirrel" in such close proximity.

So, here we are, all cloistered around the fondue pot. My two youngest are already sword fighting with their pointy, sharp forks, my teenage son is trying to see how many pieces of beef he can fit on a single skewer and still get good oil coverage, and my teenage daughter is making gagging noises about the presence of "dead cow" on the dinner table (cut in convenient cubes!). My husband keeps flinching and gasping every time one of the kids bumps the table (for some reason the idea of free-flowing hot boiling oil is of concern to him), and I'm just trying to make sure that the wine bottle is positioned more toward my end of the table.

Clearly, we've had to establish some "Fondue Rules":

1. No pushing, yelling, fighting, teasing, pinching, or poking around the fondue pot. Yes, that's right, Alex, you must leave the table until the rest of us are done.
2. Fondue forks are not to be used as duel weaponry. The end.
3. Don't lick your fingers after putting the raw meat on your fork. Yes, Nic, I know it tastes good, and, yes, Bridget I know it's what a vampire would do, but the last time I checked we were *not freaking vampires*. Mostly.
4. Double dipping is allowed, in a fondue pot. The oil will take care of any flu germs.
5. The hot boiling pot of oil (and its accompanying blue flame of fiery death) should be placed in the middle of the table, closest to those who are least likely to break into a Light Sabre Duel using the long, pointy fondue forks. (Although this is unacceptable. See rule 2.)
6. Try to find some special fondue plates—they are sectioned (sort of like a TV dinner aluminum tray) so you can keep

sauces separate from raw meats. FYI, a "sauce" can be ketchup. Truly.

7. Cut up loads of vegetables and pieces of bread to satisfy the waiting time required while cooking as well as divert any wanna-be vegans from noticing the big stack of raw steak, pork, or chicken on the dinner table. Try, anyway.

8. If at all possible, position skittery husbands away from the fondue pot. Their gasps of, "Watch out!" sudden bursts of, "Sit down!," and frantic cries of "Do you want to be disfigured for life?" can be disruptive to a friendly family meal environment.

9. You can put more than one food item on your fondue fork at a time. It is best, however, to not allow one of those food items to be chocolate of any kind.

Once the fondue is over, one of the biggest challenges is what to do with the leftover oil. Normally you will have little burned pieces of meat, mushrooms, shrimp—maybe even a fingernail—floating around in it. In England, where I last visited relatives about six years ago, this oil would simply have been added to a big metal bucket under the sink (which had been started sometime around King Arthur's day) and used every morning to fry up the eggs and sausage. Here, though, I discovered through a failing grade in my Grade 7 Home Economics class, you shouldn't pour oil down the sink. Apparently, it hardens and costs a lot of "money that could have been spent somewhere else" to fix.

If you bury it in your front yard, you'll have even more annoying dogs than usual trying to dig it up, or, in the case of one scrappy little dog in our neighbourhood, hump it. If you put it in the organics container, and then attempt to carry it to the garage, it will leak through your entire house and onto your silk pants. If you use it as plant moisturizer (hey, those leaves look dry), you're stuck again with that dog problem. I have resorted to filling perfectly good Tupperware pieces with the damn stuff and throwing it in the garbage.

Okay, that was just a joke. I don't own any perfectly good Tupperware pieces. I have about 27 lids, but that's it. I usually let the oil sit in the fondue pot for a good week, allowing the greasy smell to permeate our draperies and clothing. Then I empty a margarine container (fat out, fat in), pour in the oil, and *then* I throw it out. I'm sure there are completely non-biodegradable pots of this stuff in landfills all over Southern Ontario. But it was fun cooking over the indoor open flame, wasn't it, kids?

Leftovers--Little Pieces of Heaven

My children hate leftovers. They didn't like the food in its original format, so seeing pieces of it resurface at the dinner table a night or two later is sure to bring on great shrieks of horror and dismay. I simply remind them that if they had eaten a full plate the first night, they could have avoided this alarming revival. As much as they seem to appreciate these helpful reminders, the message has yet to sink in.

It's true that most foods are best the first time around (except cold pizza when you're hungover, am I right?). Even so, most leftover foods can also be altered. With a little creative sauce making and disguise, these leftovers are perfectly good and easy alternatives to getting a "real" dinner on the table. I often

spring a "Mommy's new creation" dinner on my poor, unsuspecting children. There were the Lasagna Stew, Maca-Pizza, and
Mashed Potato Soup; those didn't go over especially well. Now
I tend to just label all foods that have lived before as leftovers,
and skip the more descriptive names.

But before you go merrily searching through the far reaches
of your fridge, a word of caution: There are some foods that
should never achieve "leftover" status. I learned this the hard
way, through my recent attempts at Cod-aroni and Chicken a
GoGo (don't ask). Oh, and for reasons that still don't make sense,
add asparagus to this list. It's worth having this "not suitable for
reuse" conversation with your husband. Men don't seem to have
a leftover filter. They will cover and place in the fridge every last
piece of food left over on the table after dinner. "Are you gonna
eat that?" I'll ask—a question that usually has him looking at me
as if I'm crazy. So I follow up with "Do you think I'm going to eat
that? The kids?" Before he can even muster a dubious look, I rip
the offending food out of his hands and dump it in the garbage.

How Much Do I Love My Crock-Pot*?

Too much. Simply the best kitchen appliance I own—aside from
the corkscrew, that is. Now, I'd be lying if I said my kids enjoyed
the meals that come out of the Crock-Pot. But really—you've
read enough of this book by now—do you think I care? I care
that these meals are mostly nutritious, easy to make, and easy to
clean up. And Crock-Pot fare gets the kids out the door to their
annoying lessons and practices with full stomachs. My work here
is done.

Seriously, though, the Crock-Pot is a fantastic way to get dinner on the table when your day is just too full—like every day for most moms. I often find I have the most "spare time" first thing in the morning, when the kids have eaten breakfast, the lunches have been made, and I'm counting down the minutes until the school bus arrives. Throw a couple of ingredients in there, and you don't have to think about dinner again, at least for a couple of hours.

*Some people prefer the term "slow cooker" to "Crock-Pot," but I prefer the latter term. When people use the former, I always think they're referring to my mental abilities when in the kitchen.

My Just Desserts

As I've already mentioned, dessert is much more than a pleasant end to a meal. Desserts, properly handled, carry on the fine parenting tradition of bribery and deception. It's simple: Eat your dinner, get your dessert. Back in the Viking days, I'm sure little Thor was told by his mother Hildegard to eat his pickled fish before touching the sugar-coated eel. Unlike some parenting experts and Supermoms, I don't struggle at all with the concept of using food as a reward. Look, if I exercise for an hour, I feel entitled to a little treat afterward. And for my kids, getting through one of my meals can be a bit of a workout—what with the complaining, the fighting, the poking of brothers and the attempts to hide chewed food. It can all be a little tiring. Just like grown-ups trying to stick to an exercise regime, kids need a dessert "carrot" to get through the actual boiled carrots on their dinner plate.

Great, you're saying. I can barely figure out how to get breakfast, lunch, and dinner on the table, and now you're telling me I have to sort out a freaking dessert as well? Don't panic. Dessert is easy—perhaps the easiest food category of them all. First off, disabuse yourself of the notion that you actually have to make it. A couple of store-bought cookies, a scoop of ice cream, hell, even some loose chocolate chips in a bowl will do the trick for most kids. Unless you're having the boss or the snobby lady from down the street over for a meal, you most certainly don't need to knock yourself out on this course.

And the news just keeps getting better. Kids are easy to trick. For some reason, they love any dessert that comes in a parfait glass. Go to the dollar store and buy some. The glasses make every dessert seem a little fancy, and the fun factor increases when you have to dig your spoon way down to the bottom to get to the very last bite. Buy prepackaged pudding or yogurt and put it in a parfait glass with a small chocolate cookie on top. They'll go for it every time and you'll look like a hero.

And remember, they *need* this rush of sugar just before they go out to a sporting event, attempt to do their homework, or even get involved in a heavy video-game battle. You're their mother: Do it for them. Enough said.

Dinner Recipes

Dinner. Le Grande Dame of family meals. Or maybe it's just me saying, "Damn, it's dinner time" as I finish my grande Starbucks coffee. Whichever, I still have to get a meal on the table, and supposedly it should have, like, more than one ingredient. Sometimes I mix a bunch of stuff together and call it stew, and sometimes I separate the ingredients and pretend they hit a few of the food groups simultaneously. Here are some recipes to get you through dinner and onto more exciting things—like a hockey practice, a karate lesson, homework, laundry . . . damn!

Sunday Dinner Recipes

Sunday dinner becomes a lot less intimidating when you realize you don't have to cook like your mother did when you were a kid. Pretty much anything works. The objective isn't to win a culinary award; it's to get everyone around the table for at least 45 minutes. Okay, 30, tops.

Fish Cakes

Contrary to all that seems natural and right, most children like fish. Particularly a white fish like cod, haddock, or bluefish (which isn't blue, but white, trust me). These varieties don't smell too fishy, if you know what I mean. Plus, they are easy to chew—an appealing food trait for most children. This one's a favourite at my house.

Ingredients
1 package frozen fish (as above, the non-fishy-smelling-type)
4 to 6 medium-sized potatoes
Italian-seasoned bread crumbs (you can buy this, or just mix plain bread crumbs with some Italian Seasoning)
1 egg
1/4 cup milk (or to taste)
2 tbsp butter or margarine (or to taste)
salt and pepper

Directions

1. Peel and quarter potatoes (your husband could maybe even handle this part).

2. Bring a pot of water to boil (or maybe this one).

3. Boil potatoes for 20 minutes, or until soft.

4. Meanwhile, cut up fish into 2-inch pieces (it's okay if the fish is still partially frozen).

5. Place fish in a microwaveable dish, and nuke for one minute. Remove dish and stir the fish with a fork, allowing it to flake apart. Repeat, cooking and stirring in one-minute intervals until fish is cooked (usually about four minutes).

6. Drain fish and put into a large mixing bowl. Stir in the egg, and season with salt and pepper to taste.

7. Drain potatoes, and mash with milk and butter, to taste.

8. Combine potatoes and fish/egg mixture in large bowl.

9. When mixture is cool enough to touch, form into small patties. (Hint: take off your rings if you don't want to smell like raw fish all week. You might actually want to; I don't judge.)

10. Pour bread crumbs onto a plate and cover each patty with crumbs, both sides.

11. Place patties on a tray and put into the fridge for about 30 minutes. Use this half hour to pick up kids from school sporting events, detentions, and illicit smoking activities down the street.

12. Prepare vegetable for the evening meal, have a glass of wine, go the bathroom.

13. Heat vegetable oil in a frying pan at medium heat, and cook 5 to 6 patties at a time, browning both sides. This takes about 3 to 4 minutes. Note: This can throw off a lot of smoke, so open a window or turn on the fan. Or perhaps that's just the

way I cook. Tell the tallest kid to be ready to wave a tea towel in front of the smoke detector. Or do it yourself if you're like me and struggle with saggy upper arms.

14. Keep cooked patties warm in the oven in a serving dish while you fry up the rest.

15. Serve with ketchup. (In fact, I end most recipes this way: Serve with ketchup.)

Kids love these. You can also make the same recipe with chopped ham. Why not go crazy and throw in some cheddar while you're at it. There's just nothing wrong with ham, cheddar, and potatoes fried together. Oh, and maybe think about a salad or something green like that. They sell it prebagged now.

Fish Casserole

Okay, that last recipe can be a little time consuming—a good one to make while you're supervising homework or gabbing with a girlfriend. If you want to make a fish dish that's quicker, try this one. It's a great dish to use with the oven timer. It can cook while you're making that hockey-arena run.

Ingredients
1 package non-smelly frozen fish
1 large onion, sliced
1 can cream of mushroom soup (I buy this in bulk. I know it's sort of '50s, but it works)
pepper
1 cup grated cheddar cheese

Directions
1. Heat oven to 350°F.
2. Place fish fillets in bottom of 9 × 9 glass pan.
3. Place a slice of onion on each fillet.
4. Spread mushroom soup on top.
5. Sprinkle a bit of pepper on top (if the kids really don't like pepper and see every little speck as an insult to their taste buds, just skip this step).
6. Sprinkle cheese evenly on top of whole dish.
7. Bake for 40 minutes.
8. When the kids smell the fish cooking and start to complain say, "No, no, honey, it's the one fish dish you like, remember?" Kids aren't very smart so this usually works.
9. That's it! Serve with rice, since there's usually a bit of sauce.

Lasagna

Every kid loves pasta in one form or another, with sauce of one kind or another, so it almost seems like a cheat when you put it out for dinner. I'll assume you already know the "recipe" for spaghetti with tomato sauce or Fettuccine Alfredo (go to the store, buy the premade sauces—they're good, they're easy, go for it!). Instead, here's my all-time favourite lasagne recipe.

Ingredients
10 oz jar of premade pasta sauce, tomato
1 tbsp Italian Seasoning
1 onion, chopped
1 pound of ground beef
8 oz grated cheddar
8 oz grated mozzarella
lasagne noodles (8 to 10 depending on size of baking dish)

Directions
1. Heat oven to 350°F.
2. Bring water to boil in a large saucepan (*if* you are using the type of lasagne noodles that require precooking. There are noodles that you can slide right into the lasagne pan, raw. Check the label; it's bad to confuse the two).
3. Boil lasagne noodles according to package directions. Drain and rinse with cold water.
4. Meanwhile, brown the ground beef and onion together. Pour the sauce on top, and stir in the Italian Seasoning.
5. Start layering: Spread a spoonful of sauce on the bottom of

an 8 × 11 baking dish, then add noodles to cover the bottom of the pan. Spread another layer of the meat sauce, then sprinkle on the cheese. Convince one hapless child that this is something fun to do, and they will do it for you. Repeat with one more layer of noodles, sauce, and cheese.

6. At this point you can put the lasagna in the fridge to make an arena run, or put it in the oven with a timer. That will give you time to get to the train station to pick up your doofus husband who forgot his car keys at the office.

7. Bake for 30 minutes.

8. Serve and eat. Throw some cucumbers on the table to green things up.

Meatloaf Recipe 1

So many recipes, so little time! I'll be the first to admit that if you break the word *meatloaf* down into its parts—as in a loaf made of meat—it's not the most appetizing turn of a phrase. However, it *is* a great meal to make in advance, put in the fridge, and then reheat while you make that run to the neighbour's house to pick up an errant kid or something.

It's easy to chew. Kids like that. It's full-on meat. Some kids don't like that. Just tell them it's like a big hamburger without a bun and they might get into it. And get out the keg of ketchup, just in case.

Ingredients
1 lb of lean ground beef
1 egg
1 chopped onion
1 cup milk
1 cup dried bread crumbs or quick oats
salt and pepper
2 tbsp brown sugar
2 tbsp yellow mustard
1/3 cup ketchup

Directions
1. Preheat oven to 350°F.
2. In a large bowl, combine the beef, egg, onion, milk, and bread crumbs or oats. (On occasion, I've been able to convince a child to take over this messy part—until he or she

discovers that they're putting their hands in a cow's stomach, essentially. Thanks, PETA.)

3. Season with salt and pepper and press into a lightly greased loaf pan.

4. In a separate small bowl, combine the brown sugar, mustard, and ketchup. Mix well and pour over the meatloaf.

5. Bake for 1 hour. Easy frigging peasy.

Meatloaf Recipe 2

Ingredients

1 lb ground beef

1/2 cup dry bread crumbs

1 egg

1 tsp minced garlic

1 dash Worcestershire sauce

1/3 cup ketchup

1/4 cup packed brown sugar

1/4 cup pineapple pieces

Directions

1. Preheat oven to 350°F.
2. Mix the ground beef, bread crumbs, egg, minced garlic, and Worcestershire sauce. Press into slightly greased loaf pan.
3. Bake for 30 minutes.
4. Drink a glass of wine, call a friend, and catch up on Twitter. Don't ask me why, but these steps are essential to the completion of a perfect meatloaf dinner.
5. In a separate bowl, stir together the remaining ingredients and pour over the meatloaf, then bake for an additional 20 minutes. While it's baking, you may as well finish off that bottle of wine; otherwise, it'll go off. Oooh, a new Tweet!

Meatloaf Recipe 3

Ingredients

1 1/2 lbs of ground beef

1 cup dry bread crumbs

1 tsp salt

1/4 tsp pepper

2 eggs

1 tsp dried minced onion

1 15 oz can tomato sauce

2 tbsp brown sugar

2 tbsp cider vinegar

1/2 cup white sugar

2 tsp yellow mustard

Directions

1. Preheat oven to 350°F. (Are you getting the picture yet? All meatloaves cook at this optimal temperature!)

2. Combine the ground beef, bread crumbs, salt, pepper, eggs, onion and half the can of tomato sauce. Mix well and press into that loaf pan you keep using for meatloaf. Cleaning it first is optional. Sorta like the BBQ, right fellas?

3. Bake for 40 minutes.

4. Meanwhile, in a small saucepan over medium heat, combine the remaining ingredients. Bring to a boil. Yes, this recipe kind of sucks compared to the ones above because you have to do something besides drinking wine or using your Black-Berry while the meatloaf is cooking. Oh wait, I'm talking to moms—we know how to do all sorts of things one-handed

(a remnant from the baby-on-hip days). Go for it!

5. Pour the sauce over the meatloaf and bake for an additional 20 minutes (yes, this is also a pretty standard step for these loaves of meat).

Easy Easy Easy Chicken and Rice Casserole

Another perfect recipe for the times when you have to drive a child to a lesson but want to have something hot in the oven when you get home. Or, better yet, why not put in the oven with the timer on and have it ready and waiting for hungry hubby while you're on your second glass of chardonnay at the bistro down the street with the girls.

Ingredients
1 cup uncooked rice
1 can condensed cream of chicken or cream of mushroom soup (told you—bulk buy!)
1 7/8 cups water
1 package of dry onion soup mix, or 1 can of French's Original French Fried Onions*
4 skinless, boneless chicken breast halves

Directions
1. Preheat oven to 350°F.
2. Spread rice in the bottom of a 9 × 13 inch baking dish.
3. Rinse the chicken, pat dry, and place on top of the rice.
4. Mix the soup and water together and pour over the chicken and rice, evenly. Sprinkle the onion soup or French Fried Onions on top.
5. Cover and seal tightly with foil. Bake for 1 hour and 15 minutes.

*French's Original French Fried Onions are one of the great discoveries I made while working at Reckitt & Colman, in the capacity of Assistant Product Manager, Spices. These are fabulous, crunchy little onions, terrific in casseroles, or just heated up on a baking sheet for a few minutes and devoured as a snack. *Love* them.

Green Bean Casserole

Here's another recipe that features those great French Fried Onions—and that three-quarters of my kids love. In my house, that's a great percentage.

Ingredients
1 can French's French Fried Onions (or maybe two if you want to snack while cooking)
6 oz milk
dash of pepper
1 can of cream of mushroom soup (*wink wink*)
4 cups of frozen or fresh green beans, or broccoli, or cauliflower. These vegetables work well alone or in combination.

Directions
1. Preheat oven to 350°F.
2. In a medium-sized casserole mix all ingredients, reserving half the can of onions.
3. Bake for 30 minutes and stir. Top with remaining onions and bake another 5 minutes.
4. Serve and eat (if you're not full from the first can of onions you already scarfed—or is that just me?).

BBQ Recipes

If that little glimpse into an average barbecue experience at my house didn't scare you off, here are a few recipes to get you started on your own adventures.

Marinated Vegetables

Marinating is a big part of my barbecuing strategy: (1) It disguises vegetables kids might not normally eat; (2) any meat is good meat if you marinate it long enough; and (3) It somehow seems impressive to tell guests "Oh yes, it's been marinating for hours," with the underlying message being. "See how well prepared I am for having you dolts for dinner?"

Ingredients

About a cup of vegetables for each guest. Vegetables can include:

peppers of any kind—red, yellow, orange, green—cut into 1-inch pieces

onions—the more the merrier—cut into 1-inch pieces

broccoli—cut into bite-sized pieces

carrots—either the mini-kind, or sliced into thin lengths

mushrooms—sliced

zucchini—sliced

cherry tomatoes—while these do almost disintegrate to just the skin on the BBQ, they add a terrific taste

Italian salad dressing (non-creamy)—about 2 tablespoons per cup of vegetables)

Directions

1. Place cut vegetables into a large resealable bag or covered casserole dish.

2. Pour the salad dressing on top and stir or shake to cover vegetables.

3. Leave on the kitchen counter for at least half an hour, or half a bottle of wine (wow that was quick—slow down!).

4. Heat BBQ. Spray a vegetable basket (has holes all around it, with sides) with cooking spray *before* you put it on the BBQ.

5. Scoop vegetables out of bag/dish with a slotted spoon, thus removing excess oil. If you pour the vegetables into the basket while it's on the BBQ, you'll create quite a little grease fire for yourself. You don't have time to get those eyebrows tattooed back in, so follow my advice.

6. Cook until desired doneness, flipping frequently. Takes about 10 to 15 minutes on low heat.

Marinated Shrimp

Combine the words "marinated" and "shrimp" and you've got yourself an easy gourmet (don't pronounce the "t," you're embarrassing yourself) appetizer or light meal.

Ingredients
2 lbs frozen or fresh uncooked shrimp, peeled and deveined (or do it yourself)
1/2 cup vegetable or canola oil
1 tsp salt
1 tbsp minced garlic
1/2 tsp thyme
dash of hot sauce

Directions
1. Prepare shrimp so that you are left with peeled, deveined, tail-off raw shrimp. Whatever it takes to get you there. (Here's a hint: it's hard to open wine bottles with frozen fingers so you might want to buy the shrimp already cleaned).
2. Place shrimp in a plastic container that has a lid (if you can find a lid that fits, my hat's off to you. Have another glass of wine).
3. Mix together remaining ingredients.
4. Pour marinade over shrimp.
5. Place in fridge and let soak for at least 2 hours, or up to 24. (If you're using a marinade with lemon juice, marinate for no more than 1 hour.)
6. Heat BBQ. Spray a vegetable/seafood basket (has holes all

around it, with sides) with cooking spray, again *before* you put it on the BBQ.

7. Scoop shrimp out of container with a slotted spoon or tongs, thus removing excess oil. If you pour the shrimp into the pan, on the BBQ, you'll still create that little grease fire for yourself. Were you not paying attention during the vegetable section? You still don't have time to get those eyebrows tattooed in, do you?

8. Cook until shrimp turns pink. Careful not to overcook as shrimp will get rubbery. Cooking should take only 5 to 7 minutes on low heat, depending on the size of the shrimp.

9. Serve and be fancy.

Pork Tenderloin

Put up your hand if you think I'm going to say "marinade" again. You win. This recipe is for pork tenderloin, which (at time of press) is extremely reasonably priced and excellent on the barbecue. I have served this one over and over again to guests who keep telling me it's good; I choose to believe them.

Ingredients

2 pork tenderloins, approximately 2 lbs each
1/4 cup soya sauce
1/4 cup oyster sauce
2 tbsp packed brown sugar
1/4 cup honey
1 tbsp minced garlic
1 tbsp minced fresh ginger root, or 1/2 tsp ground ginger
1 tbsp ketchup
1/4 tsp cayenne
1/4 tsp ground cinnamon

Directions

1. Whisk all ingredients together. Except the pork, Einstein. You thought you could whisk pork? Maybe cut back on that wine just a tad. Or maybe you're male.
2. Marinate pork for at least 2 hours, or overnight.
3. Heat BBQ, remove meat from marinade, and cook for 20 to 30 minutes. Baste and turn every 3 to 5 minutes, stopping 10 minutes before the meat is done (to ensure that all marinade is cooked).

4. Remove from BBQ and let sit for 5 minutes before serving.
5. Slice into 1/4-inch to 1/2-inch pieces to serve.

At this point in the book, something in your kitchen should be marinating, or already marinated (if you were following my slap-dash instructions to keep drinking). Let it soak in, and enjoy.

Fondue Recipes

Basic Fondue

Mazola for cooking? Okay. Bring it downstairs, honey.

Heat oil in a fondue pot (check your pot—fuel or electric—for instructions on first-time use. I don't want any lawsuits here.) If using a fuel version, you may want to give the oil a head start by heating on the stovetop. In a saucepan. Duh.

Cut up carrots, celery, cucumber, peppers, broccoli, zucchini, and mushrooms—basically any vegetable that can be eaten raw or cooked. Actually, I don't recommend the cooked cucumber (why is it that you never cook cucumbers? Are they threatened by the zucchini?) It's not actually important if the kids cook these ingredients or not; you just want them to get some fresh vegetables into their bodies.

Slice up a baguette or toss some rolls onto the table to hit the carb side of the diet. Then cut steak or pork into one-inch cubes, season if you like, and teach the kids how to get meat onto their fondue forks without licking the raw meat blood off their fingers each time. (See basic fondue rules, page 70. It's a tough lesson to learn—something to do with worms, etc.)

Also great in an oil fondue are shrimp (peel those "peel and eats"), lobster tails (awesome), meatballs (wrap the ground beef around a cube of cheddar to give the fork something to stick to—mini deep-fried cheeseburger!). Watch for my next book: *Shut Up and Exercise*.

Creamy Pizza Fondue

This recipe combines fondue with another family favourite—
pizza! No—get the visions of dipping pieces of pepperoni and
mushroom into boiling oil out of your head (although…no, it's
too greedy). This is more of a cheese fondue alternative that the
kids (if not your waistline) will love.

Ingredients
1 1/2 lbs lean ground beef
1 small chopped onion
1 tbsp olive oil
2 10-ounce cans pizza sauce
1 tbsp cornstarch
2 tsp dried oregano
1 tsp minced garlic
2 1/2 cups grated cheddar cheese
1 cup grated mozzarella cheese
1 baguette, cubed

Directions
1. Cook ground beef and onion in oil in a large frying pan, over
   medium heat, until beef is browned.
2. In a medium bowl, combine pizza sauce, cornstarch,
   oregano and minced garlic. Stir.
3. Add to ground beef mixture in frying pan and cook, stirring
   occasionally, until it thickens and bubbles, about 5 minutes.
4. Reduce heat to low and add cheese, a bit at a time, stirring
   well throughout.

5. Transfer to a fondue pot.

6. Pierce a piece of bread on your fondue fork, dip, let cool, and eat. Ahhh. Hope you wore your eating pants.

The Ghosts of Dinners Past

As far as the kids are concerned, I try to be pretty relaxed about my approach to "ghosts of dinners past." Although I try to cook up a "new" meal each night, the kids are always welcome to finish up dinner from one, two, three, maybe even four nights ago. If you don't think it smells bad, then sweetie, neither do I. Go for it. Here are some of my easiest and favourite leftover recipes.

Curry

Believe it or not, they will eat curry. Try it. I promise.

Ingredients
1–2 tbsp olive oil
1–2 cups of leftover chicken, beef, pork, or baked potatoes, cut into bite-sized pieces
1 large onion, chopped
2 large fresh tomatoes, chopped
3–4 tbsp curry paste (I prefer Pataks, and I buy the mild, which is spicy enough for this family)
rice (basmati, jasmine, or plain old converted white)

Directions
1. Heat oil in large frying pan. Add onion and meat and cook until onion is soft.
2. Add fresh tomatoes and stir until tomato starts to break down.

3. Add curry paste, to taste.
4. Cook on low heat, covered, for about 2 hours. (If cooking uncovered, add water occasionally to replace lost moisture.) Allow the smell to permeate clothing, small pets, and a 10-foot perimeter around the house.
5. Cook the rice and spoon curry on top.
6. Serve with pappadums and mango chutney (kids like these a lot). Check for them in the Indian food section of your grocery store.

Green Peppercorn-sauced Beef Stir-Fry

As I may have already mentioned, I am the Sauce Queen.* My youngest daughter, however, seems bound and determined to take on the title. I don't make many sauces from scratch—maybe the odd cheese one—but the packaged sauces that require you to add only butter, milk, or water do a terrific job of sprucing up a tired-looking piece of beef.

Ingredients

At least 1 cup of leftover beef, cut into bite-sized pieces
2 cups mushroom, broccoli, onion, celery—whatever type of vegetable you might add to a stir-fry
1 tbsp olive oil
green peppercorn sauce mix

Directions

1. Heat olive oil in large frying pan. Add beef to warm through.
2. Remove beef and saute vegetables in oil.
3. Put the beef back in with the vegetables and set on low.
4. Make the sauce according to the package directions. Pour over the beef/vegetables in the frying pan. Let simmer just a couple of minutes.
5. Serve over rice, egg noodles, or pasta.

*I feel the need to explain my weird obsessions with sauce and seasoning packages. One of my first jobs was with a company called Reckitt & Colman, which sells sauces under the French's name. I was the Assistant Product Manager, Spices—the original Spice Girl, if you will. I learned how to properly pronounce Worcestershire, and I gained a lifelong (apparently) appreciation for their line of sauce products. I lived on my own back then (*bliss!*), so they became a staple in my diet. I could sauce anything up—chicken, pork, shrimp, hell even a piece of dry toast. A marriage and four children later, and my love for sauces lives on, as my thighs can surely attest.

Crock-Pot Creations

I keep telling you, this is easy stuff. A few ingredients, a few minutes, and you're good to go.

Salsa Roast

Kids (and some seemingly strong men) can blanch at the words "pot roast." Let's face it, there's nothing appetizing about the word "pot." Okay, maybe for a few the word association is "munchies," but this is a family book. I've left the word out here, but you know what I mean. But anything with salsa in it is bound to be fun, don't you think?

Ingredients
3–4 lb beef pot roast or pork roast (and, honestly, the more fat, the better. The meat will be much more tender)
2 cups of salsa—mild, medium, or hot, depending on your preference

Directions
1. Put the roast in the Crock-Pot.
2. Pour the salsa on top.
3. Put the lid on the crock-pot and turn it on for 8 to 10 hours on low.
4. Go and have a coffee with a girlfriend. You're done.
5. Serve the roast with a bun and salad. Presto: dinner, in literally five minutes.
6. Go and have a glass of wine with your *fun* girlfriend.

Peanut Chicken

There I said it. In the same book, I've used the words "shut up" and "peanut." I know this is all quite taboo in the world of parenting right now, but the thing is, I use these words in my house with wild abandon. I am very fortunate that my children are not allergic to any type of food, and of course I am extremely careful with children who are, but in our house, peanut butter is a staple, and I like to staple it to my chicken every once in a while. My kids *love* this recipe.

Ingredients

1 cup of salsa (mild, medium, or hot depending on your preference)

1/3 cup of peanut butter (smooth or crunchy is fine)

1/4 cup of orange juice, or any type of citrus fruit juice

2 tbsp soya sauce

2 tbsp liquid honey

1 tbsp grated ginger root or 1/4 tsp ground ginger

1/2 tsp curry powder or 1 tsp curry paste

8–12 boneless, skinless chicken thighs

Directions

1. Whisk all sauce ingredients together in the Crock-Pot (see, right away, no extra pans or bowls to clean up—what's better than that?).

2. Add chicken to the Crock-Pot and mix until covered with sauce.

3. Put the lid on the Crock-Pot, turn to "low" and cook for 6 to

8 hours (always check to ensure that the meat is cooked—it will easily fall apart if it's done).

4. Serve with rice—spoon out the extra sauce to serve at the table—or just drink it at the counter.

Crock-Pot Chili

Another easy meal to put together, but you need enough time to brown a pound of ground beef. Let's be honest, folks: This takes a total of 10 minutes, so you probably have time. Go for it.

Ingredients
1 pound ground beef (duh, weren't you paying attention above?)
1 onion, chopped
1 28 fl oz can whole tomatoes
1 6 oz can tomato paste
1 19 oz can kidney beans
1 package chili seasoning (again, embrace the sauce package!)

Directions
1. What do you think? *Yes*, brown the ground beef!
2. Throw the ground beef and the rest of the ingredients into the Crock-Pot. Depending on which chili sauce package you choose, you may have to add water. Read the directions!
3. Stir.
4. Turn on the Crock-Pot. Go play tennis or whatever it is that you do during the day.
5. Serve with toast and salad. Listen to the kids whine. Go back to the tennis courts.

Dessert/Bribe Recipes

Kids love desserts, but most busy moms don't have time to make them, particularly during the week. I like to make a dessert on the weekend, when I have time, and parcel it out in miserly pieces during the week. The desserts below, though, are quick enough to make during the week—*if* you find yourself with an additional ten minutes between yelling at kids, and for some reason you don't want to use that time to open and drink a half bottle of wine. Hey, whatever, it's your choice.

Best of all, these desserts use ingredients that you can have in your cupboards, ready to pull out when you need them. I did contemplate doing a "pantry stocking" list, but seriously, who do I think I am? And do I own a "pantry"? Do you? Bet it's full of potato chips already.

Chocolate (or Marshmallow) Pie

As far as desserts go, one of my old favourites is Chocolate Pie (also known as Marshmallow Pie). This little miracle can be made in less than five minutes. Bonus: Grown-ups love it as much as kids.

Ingredients
1 package of mousse (chocolate preferred)
1 graham cracker pie crust (these puppies seem to have an infinite shelf life, so I buy them in bulk)

1 cup chocolate chips or miniature marshmallows (or go crazy and use both)

Directions
1. Make the mousse according to the package. Try not to get chocolate spatters on your white dry-clean-only blouse. (Oh, I know you're wearing it today. There's a law about that or something).
2. Mix in the chips or marshmallows.
3. Pour mixture into the pie crust.
4. Put pie into freezer for 20 minutes.
5. Serve. Genius, eh?

Apple Crisp

My kids are much bigger on the "crisp" than the "apple" part of this recipe, so I often only use 1 or 2 apples, just to keep the peace. And *it's a bribe*, okay?

Ingredients
2–4 thinly sliced apples
3/4 cup packed brown sugar
1/2 cup all purpose flour
1/2 cup oats
1/3 cup softened butter (can use margarine, but come on, butter is better)
3/4 tsp ground cinnamon
3/4 tsp ground nutmeg

Directions
1. Heat oven to 375°F.
2. Grease glass pan, preferably 8 × 8 inches.
3. Cover bottom of pan evenly with sliced apples (or at least the pieces that are left over after your kids eat them off the cutting board—for some reason fruit is ultimately more appealing when mom is trying to cook something with it, as opposed to when it's just sitting in a bowl on the counter, waiting for someone to walk by).
4. Mix together remaining ingredients (I use my hands for this). Sprinkle mixture over apples, and bake for 30 minutes.
5. Can be served with too much whipped cream or too much ice cream.

Sugar Pie

Ain't nothing wrong with those two words, I'll tell you that. My son loves this—mostly because it is *exactly* like eating pure brown sugar, in a mom-approved sort of way.

Ingredients

1 cup packed brown sugar

1/2 cup white sugar (sounds good already, doesn't it?)

1 tsp all-purpose flour

2 eggs

2 tbsp milk

1 tsp vanilla extract

½ cup melted butter

Frozen, preprepared pie crust (deep dish is best). What, you saw the word "pie" and thought I was going to make pastry? *Ba ha ha ha ha ha.*

Directions

1. Preheat oven to 325°F.
2. In a large bowl, combine brown sugar, white sugar, flour, eggs, milk and vanilla. Beat with mixer until smooth (about 1 to 2 minutes). Stir in the melted butter.
3. Pour filling into slightly thawed pie crust.
4. Place on cookie sheet and bake for 35 to 40 minutes until filling is set. It will continue to set during cooling. And even if it's a bit runny, who the hell cares? The kids will drink it up with a spoon.

A New Way to Make Jellied Tongue

"This is a new and colourful way of serving jellied tongue. The tongue is sliced and interspersed with maraschino cherries, which glisten like rubies in the jelly. Any size tongue will do; I bought a 4 1/2 pound pickled tongue."
—*Janet Peters' Personal Cookbook*, excerpted in the pages of *Canadian Homes & Gardens*, 1956

Believe it or not, my family adores jellied tongue. In fact, they often beg me to put away the ice cream and whip up this handy recipe.

Oh, forget it. I can't keep this going. Seriously, was there an old way to make jellied tongue? I just threw this in here so you'll have some ammunition when your children tell you that you make the grossest meals ever. You don't. Janet Peters does.

5
Snacks, Snacks,
And More Bloody Snacks

"When the neighbours' children come to call, the chances are they are hungry and suspect that you have something good to eat. For them the cookie jar, the dish of ice cream, and the lollipop spell fun."
—from *The Art of Entertaining*, by Blanche Hall, 1952

"No, you and your friends can't have another Fruit Roll-Up, and no, I haven't checked the granola bars to see if they're peanut-free. Get out of the cupboards and go play with something electronic."
—Kathy Buckworth, *"When-I-was-a-kid-a-snack-was-potato-chips-and-onion-soup/sour-cream-dip, only-on-a-Saturday."*

When I was a kid, and certainly when Blanche Hall was playfully shooing those little rascals out of her kitchen, the only snacks you could find in our Day-Glo kitchen were in the cookie jar—

in my house, this was a monk whose head you took off to re-
veal homemade cookies) or on the counter in the fruit bowl. It
was a nice, reasonable existence in which meals were served and
the occasional snack made its way into your day—not expected,
but rather a pleasant surprise or a special treat.

Welcome to the 21st Century

Those halcyon days are gone. In the 21st century, the "snack"
shelves in every grocery store across North America and Europe
are taking up exponentially more real estate. And in response,
the occasions on which it is deemed necessary or desirable to
have a snack has also grown exponentially. For instance, it is no
longer acceptable to turn up at the following places or events
without a snack for your children:

1. The neighbourhood park. Even if the park is two minutes
    away and, judging by previous visits, your visit will last for
    a grand total of six minutes. In fact, I now believe that the
    whole purpose of going to the park is to eat a snack outdoors.
2. Any child's sporting event. Soccer, baseball, hockey—all
    must include not only a snack, but a "snack schedule." I did
    an informal Twitter poll and found out that 99% of moms
    don't support the idea of the structured snack, yet somehow
    that 1% who do turn up at every single sports team orienta-
    tion meeting, spreadsheet in hand. I am now starting an in-
    formal "Stop the Snack Madness" campaign for my
    children's sports. The kids are not speaking to me, but it's
    worth the price.

3.   The shopping mall, an indoor playground, or any outdoor
     venue such as a zoo, waterpark, or hiking trail. The only ex-
     ception to this rule is the movie theatre, where you can con-
     veniently purchase an overpriced snack for your expectant
     child.

It's out of control, it really is. The snack culture *has* to be a
major contributor to those soaring childhood obesity rates we're
constantly reading about, yet year after year, food manufacturers
find ways to stuff new flavours, new shapes, and new syndicated
cartoon characters into brightly coloured foil packages for our
children to admire and consume after countless hours of in-store
whining and begging.

And while I am a supporter of any food category that attempts to ensure that bacon is a major flavour ingredient, I struggle with letting my children have these snacks. Inevitably, it ruins
their dinner. They don't eat, I get annoyed, and the atmosphere
found most nights at my dinner table becomes even less pleasant.
As if the "bad dinner scene" fallout isn't bad enough, the cycle of
eating at the wrong time and not eating at the right time continues through the evening. I will now share with you a case in
point.

A Conversation with My Teenage Son

Approximate time: 9:30 at night.
     Sound effects: Cupboards banging.

Alex: Mom! There's nothing to eat around here!

Me: Technically there has to be "something to eat." I spend $400 a week on groceries for you people.

Alex: The cupboards are just full of . . . of . . . of . . . stuff. Like crackers.

(The sound of silence as I contemplate the overflowing freezer full of pizzas and chicken wings, and the fridge full of eggs, cooked meat, vegetables, and cheese.)

Me: So, besides a Wendy's Baconator, what is it that you're hoping will jump out of the cupboard or refrigerator and satisfy you?

Alex: Just food. Good food.

Me: Like what, exactly?

Alex: Stuff I like, actually.

Me: *(with admirable restraint)* What stuff do you like?

Alex: Good food.

Me: Okay, we're not getting anywhere. Can I just make you a big bowl of pasta?

Alex: Perfect.

So, when is a snack not really a snack? Some guidelines that work in my house:

1. When it turns up in more than two categories of *Canada's Food Guide.*
2. When the use of utensils is required.
3. When the use of a dinner plate is required.
4. When more than three small household appliances are deployed in the preparation.

5. When the caloric intake of the snack equals the recommended daily calorie requirement for anyone over the age of 12.

Step away from the snack cupboard.....

6
Cooking with Children
Your Life, Their Hands

"First thing you know you'll be getting a complete lunch or supper for
your mother when she's very busy."
—Betty Crocker's Cook Book for Boys and Girls (1957)

"Get out of my way—you're blocking the microwave. And put that can
opener down before you hurt yourself. Go watch TV or poke someone."
—Kathy Buckworth, reporting directly from The Real World

While doing the research for this book (yes, believe it or not, I
research this stuff!), I came across some kitchen manners from
Betty Crocker's Cook Book for Boys & Girls, from 1957. Let me
share and then helpfully update these for you. Betty starts by ad-
vising children on the best way to help mom in the kitchen. And
we're off!

Betty's Rule #1: *Choose a time to suit your mother, so you won't be in her way.*
Kathy's translation: You are *always* in your mother's way. In fact, why are we focused on Mom here? Go get in Dad's way. He's at The Home Depot? Oh, okay. Just get out the prepackaged cookie dough, then, and let's get this thing done.

Betty's Rule #2: *Wear an apron to keep your dress or blue jeans clean and be sure to wash your hands.*
Kathy's translation: No, we don't own an apron, but luckily you've been wearing the same sweatpants for four days, so a little bit of flour isn't going to hurt anything. Did you Purell?

Betty's Rule #3: *Read your recipe and all directions very carefully. Look at the pictures. They tell you how to do each step.*
Kathy's translation: What have I always told you about instructions? They're simply the manufacturer's *opinion* of how things should be done. Just do it.

Betty's Rule #4: *Put all your ingredients on a tray. Then set each one off as you use it. On another tray put all the tools and pans you'll need.*
Kathy's translation: Spray the pan with non-stick spray and divide up the dough. Come on, I don't have all day.

Betty's Rule #5: *When you're through—Have you left anything out? Read your recipe again and be sure.*
Kathy's translation: How hard can this be? How did that piece of cookie dough end up on the ceiling fan?

Betty's Rule #6: *Is everything spic and span? Then your mother will be glad to have you cook again.*

Kathy's translation: Clean up this mess or you're never doing this again. Next, I'm going to teach you how to open a bottle of wine. Where's your father? Maybe I can get him to pick up a ShamWow at The Home Depot.

I really wish I could have lived in Betty's world, circa 1960. Children were tidy and well behaved, dads could be disciplined with a light tap on the hand and an "oh, you," and frankly, having an afternoon cocktail just didn't seem as seedy as it does today. From what I've heard.

While normally I don't recommend doing anything with children that involves cleanup, rules, or the potential for a visit to the Emergency Room, if you have a child who shows the least bit of interest in cooking or baking, it's not a bad thing to encourage. After all, there may soon come a Sunday morning when you're dying for a greasy bacon and egg breakfast. Play your cards right and there will be Junior—all ready, spatula in hand—willing and able to cook it up while you drink your favourite hangover remedy.

The first foray most children make into the wonderful world of cooking is with the preparation of the traditional "Mother's Day Breakfast." This frequently botched project can be somewhat doomed from the start, due to the fact that the guidance is often being provided by a well-meaning but duty-bound dad whose prime motivation is *not* to coach, teach, and lead his young prodigy into the art of cooking, but rather to avoid recriminations and an active contribution to the ever-decreasing sexual frequency scale in North America. These children are led to believe that burned toast, instant coffee, and a spilled glass of Sunny D actually constitute a meal. We must start from scratch with them. Follow my rules; or Betty's, depending on your mood and blood-alcohol level.

Baking. A Whole New Adventure

In our fast-forward world, kids still like the idea of baking with Mom, but it can be hard to fit it in between karate class, Mom's workout, delivering fundraising meat, and, ironically, grocery shopping. Cooking from scratch has become a thing of the past in most busy families' lives. Honestly, I tend to label those moms who do have time for family cooking activities as pathetic time-wasters. I will admit that this probably stems from my own concern about not being able to use a BlackBerry in a kitchen full of sticky fingers and substances that can easily ruin anything electronic.

Instead, I encourage my daughter Bridget to find her own baking gene, which I can mentor and foster from far across the kitchen, while doing some impressive work/kids multi-tasking with my handy BlackBerry or laptop. Let me be clear, when I say "bake," what I mean is allowing her to roll out some prepared cookie dough, pastry, or brownie mix that requires little in the way of measuring, mixing, blending, beating, spilling, and generally screwing up. As with most things, a child's attention span for baking is about the same as it is for that 127th stuffed toy that they absolutely had to buy during their last trip to the mall. Hit the pre-mix section of your grocery store, load up, and let

the "baking" begin. Take my advice, and stay on the other side
of the kitchen.

My laptop doesn't have an "insert" key on it anymore because of the time I had it propped on the kitchen counter and a
bag of flour fell on it. Flour that had been in the cupboard for
seven years, and just decided, I might add, to make a suicide leap
onto my laptop. Symbolic? You betcha. Lesson learned, though.
I have since learned to keep my laptop a safe distance from the
"baking cupboard,"—which at my house basically consists of a
big bag of chocolate chips and an antique bottle of vanilla. And
where my laptop is, I'm not far behind. Far out of range of errant bags of baking products.

7
Grocery Shopping
Entering into the Gates of Hell

"The only alone time I get is when I go grocery shopping."
—Most of my pathetic time-starved friends who apparently haven't heard of Starbucks, a pedicure, or a wine bar. Actually, given that criteria, not really so much friends as women I eavesdrop on at the gym.

"Sometimes I start my grocery shopping at the other side of the store, just to shake things up." —My zany rule-breaking pal and mother of three boys, Orysa. She's INSANE.

"We like to make grocery shopping a family experience."
—Some ridiculous person I no longer have time for.

If only these sentences were uttered by people testing hallu-
cinogens in the '60s. Sadly, you can hear these sentiments at any
moms' group or neighbourhood dinner party. For the record, I
hate grocery shopping. It's not true, quality alone time if you're
pondering whether or not you really need to pick up broccoli or
dodging down an aisle you don't need to be in, just to avoid that
bitch from down the street. I ran into a friend yesterday who was
laughing about the fact that when she ran into a local store at
11:00 at night because there was literally no food in her house for
her kids, she walked smack into another friend of hers doing the
exact same thing. When I mentioned that she should maybe try
online grocery shopping (more on that heavenly service later),
she said, "But I like to feel the produce, you know?" Um, no, I
don't. Not at 11:00 at night, I sure don't. Granted, there might be
quiet moments at the store when you can answer your buzzing
BlackBerry (in fact, my BlackBerry is the only kid I'll take with
me to the supermarket), or you can read about how fat the latest relapsed Jenny Craig actress is getting without having to actually purchase the magazine, but both of these things can be
done in a much more suitable environment than Aisle 3. A nail
spa, for instance.

As far as the "family experience" goes, you're freaking kidding me, right? Whenever possible, I shop alone. Bringing the
family is just more grief than I want to cope with on an ordi-
nary day. Between a husband who thinks "shopping off the list"
is daredevil behaviour, to the fighting kids, the eight boxes of
chocolate-covered granola bars (shaped like Shrek) that myste-
riously turn up in your grocery cart, to the game of Milk Bag
Toss between the teens, a family grocery-store outing is about as

much fun as a double root canal. In fact, I'm surprised more moms in general aren't streaking out of grocery stores, screaming and ripping foil packets of fruit chews open with their teeth, just before they're carted away to that nice hospital in the country.

Online vs. Real World

For years, I've been lucky enough to take advantage of online grocery shopping. I've been a convert since the days when I worked corporate and had to travel (I'd order the groceries from the airport lounge) and I'm still one today, despite the fact that the most travel I get is actually *to* a supermarket. Regardless, it's a time saver, a convenience, and, most of all, a sanity saver.

Here's the thing: Online grocery shopping is done, duh, online. Since the kids can't tell whether I'm working or checking to see if mangoes are on sale, they don't hang over me telling me what to buy. In order to ensure that they have some sort of say (democracy and all), we keep a list in the kitchen, to which they are invited to add the foods that they realize they need to eat and that we are out of. But they need to be specific. "Good fruit" is generally not enough. Rest assured, I will get it wrong. When I shop from *my* list, I am guaranteed that I will hit every item, and that the impulse buys are left to a minimum. I also don't get caught up in the ideal of only purchasing fresh fruit and vegetables, a loaf of French bread, and sausage at the store—only to come home and be willing to give my left arm for a box of fruit chews that will keep those idiot 7-year-olds quiet for just five minutes.

Sadly, much of North America does not have access to the beauty of online shopping and delivery. And even a convert like myself can find that a once-or-twice-a-week trip to the "real" grocery store is a necessity. Preferably during waking hours. I suppose for me the grocery shopping experience has two extremes. On the one hand, there's the monotonous cruise-control method of hitting all the regular milk, bread, produce, meat and cookie aisles, done alone and in a hurry to get past those screaming, ridiculous children in front of you fighting over who gets to push the cart. On the other hand are the occasions when you are the *mother* of those ridiculous screaming children, wishing you were anywhere else on the planet because isn't that the snotty mom who once told you she was never sure it was you because all blondes look alike? That, I find, is the main risk of going to the grocery store—running into neighbours who aren't close enough to be your friends, but are acquainted enough to peer into your cart and take note of the blue-icing-laden breakfast treats, the two bottles of extra-strength Tylenol, and the lice shampoo. Why is it I feel a need to explain the purchases in my cart? And why do I always make the mistake of putting the fresh fruit and vegetables at the bottom where they (1) inevitably get squished, and (2) aren't on display for those nosy neighbours? Nope, instead I seem to end up with the frozen-food-aisle purchases right on top—the pizzas, the pizza pops, the pizza bagels, the pizza roll-ups, hell if they made a pizza ice cream that'd be there, too. "Teenagers" is what I usually mumble as I skulk past these women.

French Women Don't Have Real Lives

In Europe, or certainly in France (which we visited a few years ago), the tradition still seems to be that you plan your meals and then shop daily for what you need—always fresh, of course. While we were there, my husband said, "We should do that." Clearly, he had forgotten all about our jobs, four children, house, and social life. Otherwise we *could* do this. Oh, except for the fact that we can't toddle down a country lane to a quaint little shop where you can jokingly deride the plump owner about the softness of his or her melons. *We* have to get in the huge family vehicle, drive to the megastore, and be subjected to the careless customer service of a pimply faced teen whose under ripe melons are not to be discussed with *anyone*. Plus, did I mention we have four North American–sized kids to feed? Tell you what, buddy: You want to shop daily for wonderful fresh foods? You get right on it. Good thing there's a 24-hour grocery store down the street, because you'll be finding your bliss at five in the morning, before you get on that commuter train.

But, as usual, I digress.

The fact is, we have to keep food in the house. We also have to maintain at least a basic level of nutrition. Here are some tips to make grocery shopping—weekly, I'd advise, not daily—just slightly less painful all around.

1. Really, really, investigate online grocery shopping in your area. While you will pay a nominal delivery fee, you save on other obvious and hidden expenses, such as gas, impulse items, return trips to the store for forgotten items, and, of course, your own sanity.

2. If online shopping just isn't available, check with a local store that takes email or fax orders (some have ready-made forms). This allows you to simply do a drive-by pickup, which doesn't require unbuckling toddlers from their car

seat and then trying to strap them into the grocery cart seat minutes later (they LOVE that transition, don't they?)

3. Go shopping during off hours. Do *not* go on Saturday morning at 10:00, or Tuesday night at 6:00, when everyone else in the neighbourhood is there. It's bad enough having to buy the stuff; having to stand in line with screaming kids just makes it worse. Go early Sunday morning (skip church if you have to) or late on a Friday night—only you and all the other loser parents are there.

4. On occasion, send other family members out to do the grocery shop. Husbands are a useful alternative. They not only learn where the store is located, but also might start to see why the bills for groceries are so high. Yes, a single package of fruit chews costs about $3.99. If at all possible, send him with a child (or two) so he can experience the true wonder and beauty of this delightful chore. I've heard that the only way to practise grocery shopping with children is to try to wrestle an octopus into a small bag. Sounds about right.

5. If something is on sale, and you use it, and it's not perishable, buy as many as the store will allow you to buy. Even if it's not on your list, go crazy!

The main thing women need to recognize about grocery shopping is that it plays into some ancient, anthropological instincts. Women, as we all know, were society's gatherers; men were the hunters. I am always impressed by how men have managed to transition these skills into "hunting" at the liquor store or the aforementioned Home Depot, but have entirely skipped over the grocery store. This has left it up to us—the gatherers—to fill the void. While they get to hunt for vodka and screwdrivers, we get to gather zucchini and 12-grain bread. It's not natural, but it needs to be done. It might help to remember that one day, someone will be doing the shopping for you. And cutting your food. And helping you to the washroom. Maybe we need to just get over it and enjoy this while we can.

Part II
Entertaining

"My doctor told me to stop having intimate dinners for four. Unless there are three other people."
—Orson Welles

8
Dinner and Drinks
Sounds Civilized, Doesn't It?

"To be a successful hostess you should face all situations with an orderly plan. Otherwise there will be confusion, tension, and perhaps disappointment. Your plan must be built around the number and kind of guests, the space in your home, your physical health, the amount of time you have, the cost, and your own skill and temperament. Once you have decided you are going to entertain, the invitation list is your next logical step."
—from *The Art of Entertaining*, by Blanche Halle, 1952

Dining In

Wait a minute here—is Blanche seriously suggesting that I can blame a bad dinner party on my physical health, and, better yet, my temperament? Awesome! I thought it all had to do with the actual food being served, and not washing my hair.

At my house, inviting people over for dinner works for me on several interesting and often unexpected levels.

1. I have to clean my house. If people are coming over, I have to make at least a token effort to tidy up. I don't think people outside my immediate family will feel comfortable kicking aside the Tonka truck in order to get to the toilet in the main-floor powder room. And what is that sticky thing on the floor under the kitchen table? It's been there for weeks.

2. I get to choose the menu. This gives me a lot of flexibility. I can decide to either show off in front of my guests, or serve them crap and hope they'll be grateful that I worked them into our busy social schedule.

3. I can drink without having to worry about driving or coming up with cab fare. *Hello*. This is important, since I am always solely responsible for items #1 and #2.

4. I can legitimately say to my husband, "You need to get the kids out of the house all day so I can clean and cook." Then I can quickly sweep, start thawing something frozen, and have the house to myself. This allows me to start in on item #3 well in advance of the guests.

5. I don't have to leave before I want to.

6. I seriously think the calories you consume at your own dinner party are simultaneously burned off by all the running, serving, and worrying about how your children are leaving the bathroom every time they go in there. And what your husband is laughing about every time you enter the room.

7. Next week at the bus stop, I can casually drop into the conversation a line like, "Well, at my dinner party last week..." The other moms never need to know that it consisted of

takeout food and a case of beer in the middle of the table. I love the words "dinner party," don't you? What's better than dinner *and* a party?

8. As a woman, I am aware that whom I *don't* invite to my dinner party is just as important as whom I do. You know what I mean. Stop pretending you don't.

9. I can use a dinner party as an excuse to get my husband to clean the entire house while I go to the grocery store. What he doesn't need to know is that I bought all the groceries online and had them delivered yesterday, and I'm really at Starbucks having a coffee. It's called "me time."

10. Because I'm hosting, I can get rid of annoying people whenever I want. Usually the sight of my husband nodding off on the couch will do it. Usually. Sometimes I resort to putting out an air mattress on the floor for him. Okay, frequently.

Proceed with Caution

As handy as it may be for you to have a dinner party—for all of the reasons listed above—the decision to actually forge ahead should not be made lightly. After all, any number of things can go horribly wrong. For example, I once invited some of my husband's old friends over for dinner. You know men; they're useless when it comes to staying in touch with their old crowd, so if you don't occasionally make the effort, you'll have to live with comments like, *"Why don't we see any of my friends? It's always your friends who are here."* Here's a glimpse into why that may be the case, at least at my house.

We were having a backyard barbecue, and in a splash of splendour, I decided to serve salmon instead of the usual hamburgers, steak, and hot dogs that abound in our kid-laden world. Of course, I served up the usual charred crap to the kids, but then I made my big announcement: "I hope you adults don't mind," I said in a somewhat splendiferous tone, "if we serve salmon to you instead." I have to admit that I was expecting all sorts of oohs and ahs from this largely suburban "Kelsey's is my favourite restaurant!" crowd. Instead, one guy piped up with this: "Gee, if you don't mind, I've had too much salmon lately. You have anything else?"

Seriously. What the hell is that?

So now I can't serve him the much-anticipated salmon, and I'm forced to dig through the freezer for a steak or something more un-salmon like. As I frantically thawed the steak (if one can thaw in a frantic way, I was doing it, okay?) for this ungrateful pig, I said to my husband "Really? This guy is for real? Let's have him over again soon."

According to Blanche (above), I could have just said, "Do you know what? My temperament is such that I think you're an asshole and you're eating that salmon if I have to stuff it down your throat. Hope it chokes you, you bastard."

Clearly, Blanche never had "Salmon Boy" at her dinner table. I've had other guest-related issues, too. Like the woman who insisted on bringing her own food, as she was afraid I wouldn't serve anything to her liking. No, really. And, frankly, what she brought looked a lot like dirt, so her expectations regarding my cooking must have been pretty damn low. It's possible that these expectations were not entirely misplaced, but I can usually whip up something better than dirt. Usually.

The Groundwork

Once you've decided to have the dinner party—with eyes fully open to the potential dangers, of course—do what I do and take every person up on his or her offer to bring something. I start with the courses I don't eat, and/or those I find hard to make. Dessert comes first. Then I might assign someone a salad, an appetizer, a vegetable, etc. Before long, literally all I have to do is get my husband to throw some meat on the barbecue (see Chapter 4 on why, *in this situation*, that scenario actually works).

I like to pick a theme sometimes, just to see who will rise to the occasion and attempt to fit their contribution into it. Consider it my own little Iron Chef competition. "I'm thinking, let's do an octopus theme. Jane, you're on dessert!" Come on! It's fun—and really, it's just to mess with them. What, they can't have a dinner party at *their* house every once in a while? I do regret the "Two Fat Ladies" theme I once went with. We ate so much rich food that we actually couldn't get our shoes on at the end of the night. Or at least my guests couldn't. Not that I really cared; I was going to bed.

Choosing the date is also key. Make sure to pick a day that lands within a 24-to-48 hour window of your cleaning lady's last visit, if you have one. This way, the bathrooms have a slight chance of still being urine- and toy-free. A word of advice: If you don't have young children, and you're still having this problem, seek professional help.

On the day itself, tell the kids that setting the table is a game. For extra fun, you can have them make place cards. This will not only keep them occupied and out of your hair, but also allow you to avoid sitting next to that awful woman with the wonderful husband, or to torture your own husband by making *him* sit next to her. Bonus! If you're feeling extra lazy, give yourself the chair that's farthest from the kitchen. "I'd get up, but—oh, honey, go and get the guests some more horseradish. And whip up a side dish while you're at it."

Buy a $4.99 bouquet of flowers from the grocery store and put it in the middle of the table. I don't know why, but if you have fresh flowers in the house, people assume you are the type of person who always has fresh flowers in the house. For some reason, this will reflect well on you.

Dressing for the dinner party...hmmm...a tough one. Depends on the crowd. If there is a woman you particularly want to annoy, wear your sexiest dress or top. If you're sexy, I mean. If these are people you don't really care for, first of all, why did you invite them, and secondly, wear jeans and a corporate logo T-shirt. Whatever. Just feed them and get them out of your house, right?

It's Showtime!

Okay, so your guests start to arrive. If they have any manners at all, they will be on time. This is a *dinner* party, after all, not a farewell cocktail reception for someone they don't like. I totally call my guests out if they are late, even if we are still hours away from serving dinner. This may explain why we have trouble with people coming back another time, but at least I'm eliminating the ones who annoy me. I try to put out only a few appetizers but a lot of wine and beer. This way the guests will be quite hungry for dinner, but hopefully tipsy enough to not notice the limp asparagus or overcooked meat.

If you're barbecuing, have your husband go around with a little pad and take notes about how each guest would like their steak cooked (everyone is impressed with this for some reason). Then, he can go outside, throw the piece of paper on the barbecue coals, and make all the steaks the same. No one needs to know. They'll be drunk by the time they get to dinner, remember? Pay attention.

Once all your tardy guests have arrived, lead them to the dinner table, which, if you recall, has been set by your children. This is an easy way out of having to set the perfect table. You can tell everyone that the children got the table ready (even if they didn't) and, oh, isn't it adorable the way they misspelled all the names on the place cards, even "Mom." Park yourself in your far-from-the-kitchen chair and let your guests serve their part of the meal while your husband tries desperately to uncook some of the burned meat before serving it. Get the sauce out, honey, no one will notice. Pour some more wine.

Let the conversation flow. If you realize, an hour into the meal, that you don't want these people hanging around your house all night, introduce sex, religion, and politics into the table talk. You're sure to piss off at least a couple of guests. Failing that, start swearing—particularly if they've brought preschoolers who insist on sitting on their laps.

Which brings up another point about dinner parties. If I say it's adults only, I mean it. Leave your kids at home. I don't find them adorable, and having to make two meals (even if one is just heating up nuggets) for two separate crowds, at two separate times, is a pain. Plus, even though we're supposed to be well out of the '50s, every time I either host or attend a dinner party where children *are* included, all the moms end up in the kitchen feeding the kids, clearing the table, cutting up the meat, pouring the juice, breaking up the fights—while the dads sit in another room or backyard, drinking beer and scarfing down all the appetizers. This annoys me on so many levels.

If you *must* invite children to a dinner party (your own kids likely need feeding at some point, too), then it really is best to split up the meal into two feeding sessions. Either order a pizza or throw some nuggets and fries in the oven. The kids are so overhyped from being allowed out of the house that they won't sit down and eat more than a few bites anyway. Don't make the mistake of trying to impress the other moms with your cute cutout sandwiches or nutritionally sound salads and fruit kabobs. I've done this. The kids don't eat them and the other moms will either assume you have too much time on your hands or that you're just doing it to bug them. And they're right, aren't they?

Another steadfast rule is to stop each child as they enter your house and quiz them on their allergies. Have them sign a waiver, if you have to. My children don't have a single food allergy (just ignore my teenage daughter who will claim she's allergic to anything that could have been a pet), so it's hard for me to know what to put out. I had a friend once who claimed her child was allergic to things just because she hadn't bothered to try them and it was easier that way. While I admire the Slacker Mom initiative, it is annoying when you're not sure if what you're serving the kids is life threatening or just fodder for a good whine.

And to all you moms who don't allow your children to drink pop. That's fine, I get it. But it's Friday night. My kids are allowed only one can of pop a week, on a Friday, so if they want it, they can have it. I had a mom tell me that because she didn't allow her kids to have pop, that I shouldn't let mine have it either, as it wasn't fair to *her* children. Um, you're in my house, so here's the thing: shut up.

Which brings up another inherent problem with feeding other people's children in your home when parents are around (particularly the moms, it pains me to say). It can lead to situations in which you are required to say things like

- "No, sweetie, I'm not sure why Jason has to have his meat cut in triangles with a special knife brought from home—along with his special meat, organic green beans, and flax 'just for sprinkling.' Yes, help yourself to some Cheesies."
- "Yes, that bib and special spoon and fork set little April brought along for dinner is very cute. I threw yours out when you turned two. Maybe April is just pretending she's a baby one more time before she goes into junior high next week."
- "I'm sorry, Jane, but I didn't know that you have a 'one pizza a month' rule at your house. Sure, go ahead and cook the kid an omelette if you want. Let me just get the four-course meal for the adults off the stove for you. No, it's no trouble."
- "Yes, Bob, I understand that setting up a separate table at which the children can eat without us could seem a little autocratic and demeaning, but you need to understand this: shut up."
- "No, honey, I don't have the special kind of ketchup that your mom makes herself. But I'll give you a tomato and a hammer, if you'd like."

Please don't get me wrong. Generally speaking, I love having people over for dinner. I especially love having people over who ignore my messy countertops, mismatched bathroom towels, overflowing cupboards, and slightly spotty wine glasses. I've realized that if I have a guest in my house who goes into my cupboard looking for a bowl and I get nervous about what they'll find in there (Lego, used wet wipe, dead bug) this is likely someone I'll have to end my friendship with. Take me as I am.

The Other Side of the Coin

Of course, having people to your own house is only half the fun! Sometimes we're lucky enough to be invited *out* for a dinner party. I don't know if dinner parties in general are on the wane, or if it's just *our* invitations, but this doesn't happen as often as it used to. (I prefer to think it's a downward trend in general. These blinders I have on aren't just for my parenting issues, okay?) Still, I've been to some terrific dinner parties—scintillating conversation, great food, lots of wine, memory loss . . . you know. Unfortunately, I've also been to some that left me wondering why the host bothered to have one in the first place, and why we decided it would be a good thing to go.

A case in point. We were once invited to dinner at an old friend of my husband's—which should have been a red flag right away, honestly, as old friends of husbands inevitably turn out to be people with whom most wives will not want to hang out. (This is a theory, by the way, that I've seen proven over and over. If you doubt me, refer back to the Salmon Boy story near the beginning of this chapter.) Anyway, at the appointed hour—and yes, you guessed it, we were on time—we arrived at this friend's house in a trendy part of downtown Toronto. Our suburban sensibilities had allowed us enough time to get to the city, and we naively expected our guests to be expecting us at five o'clock, as they had invited us for five o'clock. Upon our arrival, we were greeted by the news that they both needed to go upstairs and have a shower, and, oh, could we watch their two kids while they did that? Yep, liking these guys already, honey! Let's allow another 20 years to go by before we see them again, alrighty?

So as my husband and I opened our own bottle of wine and stood in the kitchen watching our children and theirs manoeuvre themselves around the dog-poop minefield in their backyard (which, I have to admit, was worrying me as I thought they might ask us to clean up while they dressed), their great huge stupid dog jumped up to the counter, grabbed one of the marinating steaks (the only sign that they were, in fact, expecting us for dinner) off a plate, threw it down his throat in one gulp, and left. I turned to my husband and said:

"Were we supposed to be responsible for that, too?"

As the couple re-entered the kitchen, freshly showered, I laughingly told them what the dog had done. The husband turned to his wife and said, "It's your stupid dog. No steak for you I guess, eh?" He turned to us and said, "I refuse to pick up that dog's shit, as well." *This* we knew. He proceeded to pull a hot dog out of the fridge, which he spitefully cooked up for his darling wife to eat at dinner. He didn't notice me and my husband surreptitiously cutting off parts of our steak to feed to the poor woman. Wow, once you've been to a dinner party that bad, you can only go up.

Which brings me to my final point. Just like we all decided we had to perfect the art of parenting, we've all apparently signed some unwritten agreement about being the perfect host. Many women I know are now hesitant to throw their own dinner parties because they think the effort has to be worthy of a spread in a Martha Stewart magazine. Trust me when I tell you, it doesn't. Buy the wine, thaw some steaks, and, believe it or not, you're halfway there. Invite the right guests (i.e., not your husband's friends) and you might even have some fun. Arm yourself with this knowledge, and you'll find you're fresh out of excuses. Listen, it's not that you're too busy—you had time to get to the grocery store alone, didn't you?

Cocktail Parties

"I misremember who first was cruel enough to nurture the cocktail party into life. But perhaps it would be not too much to say, in fact it would be not enough to say, that it was not worth the trouble."
—Dorothy Parker

You got it, Dorothy. Like the family dinner, the classic cocktail party has a mythical reputation: sophisticated ladies, dapper men, brightly coloured martini glasses with jaunty olives and the soft tinkling of a piano in the background. Even smoking was cool then. (They had silver boxes of cigarettes out on tables and everything.)

Now come to my house. Cackling women fighting over the children's Cheesie bowl, a child running by with a broken skateboard threatening to whack another child over the head while yelling, "Mommy says bad words so I can too," the husbands sneaking out back to barbecue and talk about sports. And there are always at least one or two moms trying to sneak a smoke in my garage before the kids notice they're missing. The takeout pizza is congealing on the dining room table and the dessert that took me 30 minutes out of my way today to pick up will be forgotten and left in the downstairs refrigerator for at least six months.

Sadly, it seems that parents who just want to have other parents over in the neighbourhood for a quick drink—i.e., a cocktail party—are unable to do so these days unless they extend the invitation to their children. If you even attempt to broach the whole "adults-only" topic, you may hear something like this: "Oh, I'll just put them in front of the TV. It'll be no trouble. It's just not worth the hassle of getting a sitter for a couple of hours when we'll just be down the street."

Ummm, yes, it is. It is totally worth the hassle.

Children like to sit in front of the television only if they are supposed to be doing homework, cleaning their room, or performing some other required domestic task. They don't like watching TV when Mommy and Daddy are trying to have an adult conversation in the next room, especially one in which they don't have to censor themselves from saying awful words like "stupid" and "shut up."

Children *like* to be around adults when adults are drinking. I'm not sure what weird law of nature prescribes this, but there it is. The minute you have your lips on a cold glass of Pinot grigio, there they are, asking for snacks, Lego kits they haven't played with in three years, and the arts and crafts equipment. You're thinking the following thoughts:

1. Go away. Mommy has a glass of wine and if she doesn't get to drink it she will run away from home.
2. Perhaps if you looked after your toys instead of whirling them about the family room like a maniac, you'd know where to find them when you have friends over and I wouldn't have to stop drinking the aforementioned wine.
3. Yes, you can have snacks. Take whatever you want. I don't care if it rots your teeth, makes you fat, or gives you high cholesterol. Make sure you give some to that whiney neighbour kid with the overbearing mother just so I can watch her freak out when he bites into an Oreo Cakester. Pair that spectacle with my nice glass of wine and that's what I call dinner and a show, bud.
4. Arts and crafts equipment? Are you freaking kidding me? If you're lucky, you'll find some glue, a broken zipper, and a soggy egg carton in that box in the basement. Go make yourself a Madonna bra or something.
5. Do whatever you want, but first hand this list of neighbourhood babysitter phone numbers to that kid's mom. She needs it. Tell her I'll pay for the first session.

Bringing your kids to a cocktail party is cheap and annoying. Please don't do it. Get a sitter or don't come. We don't think your kids are adorable when they're eating all of the olives, drinking apple juice out of a crystal wine glass, or turning off the soft jazz and putting on the soundtrack from the latest Pokémon movie.

Getting It Done

Some people think it's necessary to clean their homes prior to any type of party. Not so. For example, this is 100% *not* true if you are having a child's birthday party—it'll be messy within seven seconds of the guests' arrival, and honestly, if they are the type of children who care about a messy house, do you really want those freaks hanging out with your kids? The cleanup required for a cocktail party is also, I think, minimal. Let's review:

1. Most cocktail parties take place after the sun has gone down. Throw some candles on the tables, turn off the overheads, and you're good to go.
2. These people are at your house because *they want to drink*. If they have ulterior motives such as pleasant conversation and home décor discussions, you need to change some of those friends for normal human beings.
3. Any parent (and let's face it, these are basically the only friends you have left) is just so happy to be out of the house *without their kids* that they're going to make a beeline for the drinks. They are not going to stop to ponder why you have 18 school forms and 27 knapsacks lying in your front hall.
4. Normally, by the time they need to go to the bathroom they've had a few drinks, so they'll never really be sure it wasn't *them* who left the dirty handprints on the towel or missed the bowl by just a tad. (Yes, this can be disturbing for your women guests, but whatever.)
5. While I fully advocate not allowing other people's children to come to my house during a cocktail party, I normally try to have a couple of mine lurking around. A few well-placed

comments—"Bridget, I told you not to get that painting set out now" and "Nicholas, did one of your friends play with the Lego this afternoon?"—and your guests will never know that the offending items have been sitting on your dining room table since 1998.

6. If you raise the bar in terms of cleanliness at your house, you put a lot of pressure on these other lovely people to do the same. Take pity on them and let them have a bit of superiority over your cleaning skills. It's worth it.

7. Are you one of those people who is always saying "I'm so busy!"? (And really, who isn't? Do you know anyone who complains about having too much time on their hands?) It's hard to justify this position if you somehow found the time to wipe down the baseboards or organize the shoes in the front hall. *That's* what had you so busy? Really? Hmmmm.

So, we're making some progress here. We've established there is no place for children at a cocktail party, and that your house doesn't have to be all that clean. The next step is managing your guests. It is important to let your guests know their expected time of arrival. It's okay to arrive fashionably late: If the invitation is for 7:00, they can easily slide in up until 8:30. If they should, however, decide to go out for dinner first, catch a movie, and then drop in, I'm going to be a little pissed. They're going to turn up in time for the party's second wind, which is just about the time I want everyone but the really fun people to leave my house. If you're turning up at 10:00, trust me, you're not one of these people. You've probably also spent the last two hours over dinner with other guests, talking about how messy my house is going to be, and how annoying it is to pay a sitter when you could have just brought your darling angels along with you.

Whatever.

Along with establishing clear time expectations, it's important to remember that most people who come to your party are there to drink. Hello, it's a cocktail party. Make sure to set up a bar on a kitchen table or counter. This will imply that your guests should help themselves at any time, and not wait for you to repeatedly ask if they need their glasses filled. My drunkard friends normally like to establish a comfortable standing or seating stance quite near the makeshift bar, so as to be first to know when their drink of choice is running out. I support this behaviour, of course, and have been known to provide extra seating in and around the kitchen, just for this purpose. You should also prepare a bowl of non-alcoholic punch for those guests who will be in the driver's seat later in the evening. But you smart moms already knew that. Now go get a real drink.

Dinner and Cocktail Party Basics

Just because you're having people over for dinner doesn't mean you have to stray from your regular protein-veggie-starch combo. In fact, it works quite well.

Quick and Easy Protein

- The easiest dish to make is always something roasted—if you can't convince the BBQ King to do his thing, that is. Roast beef, roast chicken, roast pork—it's all the same. Throw on some seasoning, stab in a meat thermometer and sit down for a precompany cocktail. You're good.

Quick and Easy Vegetables

- A prewashed, precut bag of salad. Doesn't get any easier than this. Fancy it up by adding some slivered almonds, raspberries, and goat cheese. You're a star!
- Roast vegetables: Wash and cut up asparagus, broccoli, or green beans. Marinate in a resealable bag with olive oil, salt, and pepper for at least 20 minutes. Heat the oven to 400°F, put the vegetables on a baking try and bake for 15 minutes, turning once. Crispy and good.
- BBQ vegetables: Wash and cut up peppers, onion, zucchini, broccoli, cherry tomatoes, and carrots. Marinate for at least

20 minutes in a resealable bag with olive oil and balsamic vinegar, or a prepared oil-based Italian dressing. Spray a BBQ vegetable basket with non-stick spray (before putting on the BBQ, if you value the hair on your arms and your eyebrows), scoop out the vegetables from their marinade (don't pour them in as the oil will catch fire, doofus), and cook until done. Complete this task ahead of time and heat up the veggies in the microwave, or serve at room temperature. Honestly, I don't care.

Quick and Easy Starch

- Your easiest choice is a fresh loaf of artisan bread served with butter and/or olive oil and balsamic vinegar. Many people like to avoid carbs (or let's just say many of them *should* avoid them) so no sense knocking yourself out here).
- Rice: Rice is easy to make—either regular long grain, basmati, or jasmine. Throw some Italian Seasoning and a drop of lemon juice in the water while it cooks and the rice doesn't look quite so plain. This buys you time to make yourself look a little fancier, too.
- Baked potatoes: Wash, pierce, nuke. Done. Putting sour cream, real butter, and some chives or bacon bits on the table suggests that you made an effort.

Salmon for People We Like

This is a great salmon recipe for people who actually like it. And my advice? Don't ask, don't announce—just serve.

Ingredients
Cedar plank (most grocery stores carry them, or grab something from the remnant pile next to your new fence; however, do not use any type of treated or softwood)
4 salmon fillets (each about 6 oz and 1 inch thick)
4 tbsp olive oil
4 tbsp finely chopped shallots or red onion
fresh dill
1 lemon, cut in half
coarsely crushed black peppercorns
coarse salt
coarse language (for that bastard who doesn't want it)

Directions
1. Overnight, soak the plank in water—weigh it down with one or two cans of food to keep the wood submerged.
2. Smack anyone who deserves it (i.e., anti-salmon guy) with the plank.
3. Preheat grill to high.
4. Rub the salmon with the olive oil and sprinkle with onions/shallots and black peppercorns.
5. Sprinkle each fillet with a few sprigs of the dill and squeeze some lemon juice over top.
6. Place plank on grill and sprinkle with coarse salt and coarse

language if you're still mad. Heat with the cover closed for 2 to 3 minutes, or until plank is nearly dry.

7. Place salmon fillets on the plank. If you have a two-burner barbecue (ooooh, fancy aren't we?) turn off one burner and place the salmon on that side. If you only have one burner (awww), turn the heat to the lowest setting.

8. Cook the salmon for 10 to 12 minutes, until cooked through and flakey.

9. Squeeze more lemon juice on top and serve.

10. Throw the steak at that idiot. Don't cook it if you don't want to. He might need it for the black eye you gave him with the plank.

Crab Dip

For some reason, the inclusion of crab in any appetizer dish makes people think you're sort of fancy. I'm not talking about producing a crab puff or anything ridiculous like that, but merely a small, delicious crab dip that takes minutes to put together.

Ingredients

1 6 oz can crab meat
1 8 oz package of cream cheese
2 tbsp milk
2 tbsp horseradish
2 tbsp lemon juice
crushed red or cayenne pepper

Directions

1. Unless you want to get some extra arm work in because you missed a session at the gym, take the cream cheese out 30 minutes ahead to soften. Make sure your ever-helpful husband doesn't keep putting it back in the fridge when he walks by. *Ha ha ha.* Sorry, that was a joke—since when do men put things *back* into the fridge?
2. Once the cream cheese has softened, and you've stopped laughing at my last joke, drain the crab and discard the juice. If your kids are up for a game of Toddler Fear Factor, get them to drink the crab juice.
3. Mix all ingredients until well combined. Have another glass of wine (what, you haven't had one yet and you have people coming over tonight? Are you crazy?). Sprinkle the red pepper on top.

4. At this point, if you need to run a child to a birthday party or have a shower or do something productive, you can cover the dip and put it in the fridge. When you're ready (no, no really, take your time), heat in a 350°F oven for half an hour.

5. Serve with carrot sticks and celery (really any dipping vegetable), or crackers and bread if you have friends who can take the carbs.

Bacon Wrapped . . . Well . . . Anything

Everyone loves bacon. Really. Even vegetarians, I believe, would try to sneak a BLT into their last meal. It stands to reason, then, that anything wrapped in bacon is, by mere association, good. Here are some terrific things to wrap in bacon, cook and serve at your next cocktail party.

canned smoked oysters or mussels
water chestnuts
shrimp
scallops
cheese (cook the bacon separately—cheese melts)
cherry tomatoes
mushrooms
olives
a rock

Non-Alcoholic Punch

It is likely that half your guests will choose not to drink because they are the designated driver. Bravo. We need to make these selfless folk feel like they're getting a little something for their effort besides peanuts and crab dip. I usually prepare this punch, which not only appeals to my retro side, but makes it look as though I've "made an effort."

Ingredients
2 litre bottle of ginger ale
2 litre carton of orange juice
1 litre bottle of cranberry or grape juice
Maraschino cherries and orange slices

Directions
Um, what do you think? Just mix it all together, Einstein.

Everything's Relative
Feeding the In-laws and Outlaws

"People who might not find one another very interesting at a small dinner, can be relied upon at a crowded cocktail party to find each other moderately entertaining."
—Janet Peters, *Personal Cookbook* (1952)

"People who might not find one another very interesting can be relied upon to be related."
—Kathy Buckworth (including myself in that, 2010)

Okay, you have to have them over. They're relatives. You're related. One of them gave birth to you or your spouse, another shared a room with you, and yet another gave you a scar you still carry today. Because they care about you (or maybe just your kids), occasions will arise when you must welcome these people into your home. We're talking about things like birthdays, anniversaries, holidays, and other heart-warming family moments. Whatever the *raison du jour*, you'll want to put out some food that shows you have it all together (to make a point, of course). But here's the thing: if you put out something *too* fancy they're likely to either turn up their noses or make some annoying remark about how you clearly have nothing better to do with your time than experiment with haute cuisine (like raise their unbelievably rude grandchildren, for example).

You can't really win here, so why not stop trying and save yourself a bit of time and sanity? For example, you do want to put out an appetizer that shows you know what a fresh vegetable looks like. Do yourself a favour, though, and stop short of spending a fortune or visiting a specialty boutique across town to pick up hard-to-find ingredients. Even with these self-imposed limits, you can still make something that looks like you went to the effort and is fancy enough for *your* mom to brag about—"She's so clever!"—and for *his* mother to throw in her other children's faces. (Like the time we brought store-made sushi as our contribution to an in-law family dinner. "It's from my Toronto son," his mother proudly exclaimed. See what I mean?)

Setting the Stage

Getting ready for an extended-family dinner is similar to getting ready for an average dinner party. I use the old "get the kids to make the place cards" trick here, too. You know whom you want to sit next to (and whom you don't), and you know whom not to place your nose-picking 7-year-old beside. Or on whom to force him.

Unlike at dinner parties, kids can be quite useful at family gatherings. Chances are good, after all, that the relatives are more interested in seeing the offspring than in seeing you. A word to the wise, however, before you yank the power cord on their game system and haul them into the land of the living: Try to evaluate issues of personal hygiene and general demeanour with a dispassionate eye. Depending on the life stage of the child in question, an extended trip to a friend's house may be in order.

Once you've weeded out the potential troublemakers, try to ensure that the remaining progeny are able, at some point, to demonstrate that you have at least attempted to raise them like human being, not wolves. This can be particularly tricky with teenage boys, who scowl and smirk and slouch their way through every day. On reflection, however, it might be equally worrisome to have the "outgoing" one turn up in Spock ears to show Granddad his latest acquisition from the Star Trek convention. There's really no winning with this age group.

Little kids are generally fine to put on display, but try to make sure they (1) understand the punishment procedure for saying "asshole," (2) remember not to remark on the strange growth on the side of Grannie's head, and (3) don't utter random sentences about killing their brother while he sleeps.

The best offspring to put on display with relatives are, hands down, the babies. Stupid baby tricks are *always* a hit, and if you're only having your side of the family over, you can always blame the unfortunate bad looks on his side. Having baby sit, clap, crawl, roll over, or even blink can be great fun if you do it with your own siblings, whose children are much older. You'll both know how lame these demonstrations are, but the grandparents will eat it up and you can slide once again into "favourite" position. Well played.

But all the "staging" in the world can't save you from that moment—you know, the one where you have to sit down and actually eat. Once you've gathered the masses at the family dinner table, don't be at all surprised to hear phrases like these thrown around:

- "Oh, is that how you make the gravy, Kathy? All these years and I never thought to buy a package mix. Aren't you smart? Good thing my son makes so much money."
- "Do you have any *real* salad dressing? Like Kraft Thousand Island?"
- "Where's the ketchup? The BBQ Sauce? The mustard? The horseradish? The relish? The mayonnaise? The sour cream?" (Just take my advice and load every condiment you have onto the table beforehand. Who cares?)

In order to deflect these and other nasty comments, be sure to preload your husband with appropriate phrases about how busy you are with (1) work, (2) the children, and (3) the house. Not only will these witty comments divert attention from the food, but also fend off the "what could keep her so busy all day" rumours. Before everyone arrives, remind Hubby Dearest whose side he's pretending to be on. He can call his mom later, after you've gone to bed.

The Holidays: Extreme Eating Events

As if preparing a family meal isn't hard enough during a regular week—which typically consists of 40 hours of work; 16 hours of driving; up to ten scheduled sporting or after-school events; three visits to some sort of medical practitioner; 17 trips to the grocery store, sports equipment depot, and/or suburban mall; and a disturbing incident with a teacher of some kind—every few months we have to whip ourselves up into a feeding and entertaining frenzy known, ironically, as "the holidays." Or, as I like to call them, "Extreme Family Bonding Events." Year after year, for some unknown reason, we convince ourselves that this will be the "best one" ever—best Christmas, birthday, Halloween, Groundhog Day, whatever. And year after year we are somehow surprised to discover that with all of the extra hype, activity, and lack of sleep, our family bonding moments have become more stressful than ever. And the food? Well, can we talk about the food? Of course we have to. The food at most holiday tables is a crazy assortment of traditional family recipes, a new experimental and trendy twist (remember when everyone was putting live flowers on their salads—why, people, why?), something dried out, and something overcooked. Sort of a something old, something new, something borrowed and, if you choose meat like I do, something blue kind of approach. The result? One twisted family meal.

The holidays themselves have gotten blown out of all proportion in recent years (I blame Kathie Lee Gifford, not sure why). You can now buy Halloween lights, Easter eggs to hang from trees to make Easter trees (an ancient Christian practice,

I'm sure), and turkey hats, tablecloths, and napkins for Thanksgiving. I'm waiting for the first mom to turn up at the school with freaking Groundhog-themed cupcakes before I really lose it.

Have Yourself a Merry Little . . . Oh, Whatever

Despite the entry of these new "faux" holidays into the pantheon of events for which we all must prepare, and shop, and suffer, one occasion still reigns supreme—the king of the holiday jungle, if you will. Oh, yeah. You know what I'm talking about. Christmas.

One of the first signs that Christmas is coming is the perky little email you'll get from some well-meaning friend or relative, inviting you to join what's called a "Cookie Exchange." This is a very frightening ritual where women throw down their briefcases, stethoscopes, even BlackBerrys, to immerse themselves in the baking of special little treats—about 140 of them, at last count. The idea is that you share the results with like-minded women, allowing you all to have some "Christmas baking" in the house. Gird your loins, ladies (not, by the way, quite as easy or sexy as it sounds).

The real purpose behind having Christmas baking in the house is not clear, as most women will spend the balance of the year complaining about the size of their own thighs and the expanding girth of their husband. (Note to editor: Didn't think I could fit "gird" and "girth" into a two-paragraph space, did ya? *Impressive—ed.*). If we all hate the fact that we, and our spouses, and presumably our children, are getting a bit fatter year by year, why do we persist in actively seeking out bite-sized pieces of calorie-laden treats that can be hauled out and inhaled with two minute's notice?

I'll also admit to finding something strange about actually *wanting* to make 140 little macaroons or confetti squares. Don't you people have a better way to spend your afternoon? Like filing your nails? Regrouting the bathroom tile? Watching paint dry? And let's face it, because of the above-mentioned weight-gain worries, you know most of those treats are going straight into your husband's mouth—and ladies, aren't we now finally past the stage of caring whether we get to his stressed heart through his overextended stomach? I say stick to the holiday drinking and let the nice lady down the street drop off some after she realizes that no one else has joined in the madness, and she's already baked a million little macaroons.

To be fair, this urge to bake simply cannot be suppressed in some people. Use it to your advantage. These are, after all, the same women who routinely send you emails about joining a Recipe Exchange. I usually just send them a note inviting them to find out about this wonderful new thing called the Internet, where you can look up *any* recipe you want *anytime* you want.

The next sign that Christmas and all of its food implications are lurking just around the corner is the first signs of organizational efforts for the annual Family Christmas Dinner. His family, your family, the families of ex-spouses who still want to see the kids, even if they wish you'd drop off the face of the earth. Hey, singletons, here's some advice: Seek out someone who doesn't celebrate Christmas, for whatever reason. You'll halve the pain that way.

So what, you're thinking? A lot of families go back and forth between the in-laws for Christmas. What's so bad about that? I suppose the answer would be "nothing," if that was the only challenge. But remember folks, before you can even get to the hell that surrounds those travel logistics, you've got to wade through the minefield know as menu planning.

For years, I was not asked donate a dish to my in-laws' Christmas dinner. While not insulted (hey, less work for me), I was a little curious. One day, I asked my husband about it. He said he had honestly never thought about the fact that his parents, his two sisters, *and* his brother's wife had been bringing tons of food to the Christmas dinner table each and every year while neither he nor I had been asked to contribute a thing.

So the conversation with the husband clarified nothing. Big surprise there, huh? I thought about it a little more on my own, and couldn't decide whether it was my personality or my cooking that was scaring them off. Either way, it didn't appear as though an invitation to start pitching in from our end was coming any time soon. But, finally, one year—and probably due to some sort of desperation on their part—I was awarded a contract to supply a truly special part of the Christmas dinner: The children's dessert. (Because really, how much could I screw that up?)

I decided to prove something to all of them. The point of that escapes me now, but that first year I made goody bags, *and* individual little cakes, decorated with sparkling snowmen, smiling Santas, and candies. After about three years of repeat performances, I asked if I could perhaps be promoted to some other dinner-related duty; something that might make an appearance on the grown-up table. Initially, my request was met with a hushed silence, but finally I was told that I could, in fact, make the potatoes—The Christmas Potatoes. And yes, the capitalization is required. You'd know why if you'd met any member of this family.

"Oh," I said, pleasantly surprised. "I have some great recipes for potatoes."

That hushed silence quickly became a stunned silence. "No, no, you have to make The Christmas Potatoes," one of his sisters finally ventured. "We'll give you the recipe."

Okay, now I got it. I could make the potatoes *only* if I followed *their* recipe. In the interests of full disclosure, I should note that it's a very good recipe that involves sour cream, so really, how could a person go wrong? I made them, and thankfully they were well received. I liked them so much, in fact, that I made them for the following year's Easter dinner.

Now, it may seem obvious to some of you that this was a complete faux pas, but I honestly didn't realize that The Christmas Potatoes could only be made *at Christmas*. I know now— and yes, I'll be back to making the children's dessert for Thanksgiving.

What's the Deal with the Bunny and the Eggs?

Easter has always been one of those holidays that sneaks up on me. I'm not religious, so the whole Good Friday thing doesn't really remind me that in a couple of days I'm going to have to hide sticky chocolates and jelly beans in my perfectly unsticky living room. I will confess that one year, having bought the candies early in a hitherto unseen fit of organization, I totally forgot to play Easter Bunny and hide them. (This happens to other parents too, right?) So while my husband literally blocked off the children at the top of the stairs, telling them he thought he heard an intruder (hey, yes, why not give them nightmares, all in the name of perpetuating yet another parenting lie), I hurled chocolate eggs into every corner of the room I could reach from the bottom of those same stairs. Honestly? The kids were ecstatic to find eggs outside their normal hiding places, and the preparation took way less time than usual. This technique is highly recommended.

Sometimes, the whole Jesus thing actually does get wrapped into the festivities at our house and, frankly, I have a hard time separating the stories. At this point, I'm pretty sure that my youngest child believes that the Easter Bunny delivers chocolate but God bestows the jelly beans. Whatever works, eh? It's the same philosophy that gets us all through the "fun for the whole family" game playing after those family holiday meals.

Gobble, Gobble

There are many things to be thankful for when you have children. Here are some that might occur to you, as they do to me, while you're sitting around the Thanksgiving dinner table with your extended family:

- Your son didn't wear his FCUK T-shirt to the dinner table. Grandparents still consider it offensive. And so do I, on a certain level at least.
- You decided against serving the peas. (You've eyeballed at least two slingshots peeking out of shorts pockets.)
- Your kids use so many slang/rap expressions when dissing each other that your parents don't really know what they're saying. Including "dissing."

- Your mom decided to serve dinner buffet style, so the kids can choose what they like. One piece of broccoli and four pieces of bread? Fine. Don't care. Sit down and shut up—instead of complaining about their plates full of things they won't eat. Otherwise, you'd get blamed for both wasting food and not raising your children properly for. Or is that just me?
- Candied yams are considered a *vegetable* and not dessert. How (literally) sweet is that?
- It's a special occasion, so the calories don't count.
- Turkey contains tryptophan, which is known for inducing sleep. You will have a lovely, quiet car ride home if you have an extra coffee and load up hubby's and children's plates.

One of the best things about Thanksgiving is that it's a really short holiday. Basically, it lasts for one meal (at least here in Canada, where we do it on a Monday in October, with no real football games or pre-Christmas shopping frenzies to attend to). Other festive occasions that are mercifully only a day long are children's birthdays and Halloween. The birthdays seem longer because you have to spend so much time planning them, but the actual event is mercifully short. Likewise Halloween. And the *really* good news about Halloween is that you don't have to bother making dinner that night, or breakfast the next morning. It's all about the candy. And even if you are the type of parent to force your kids to eat something healthy before they go out trick or treating, rest assured that they'll shove any nasty dinner down their throat just to get out there. Score.

So my advice is to take the holidays as they happen, and to try not to get too stressed about the food that needs to be purchased, prepared, cooked, and eaten. The tradition of these meals has been going on a long time, and it's going to take more than you making Christmas Potatoes at Easter to ruin it for everyone. I think.

Family Dinner Favourites

Part of the reason these recipes ended up in my "favourites" section for family dinners is because they are so easy to put together, you can literally do make them with one hand tied behind your back—or simply pre-occupied with something else . . . like holding a glass of chardonnay, for example. (I would suggest you don't hold that behind your back; it makes for difficult quaffing.)

Red, White, and Toasted All Over

The name of this recipe applies to the appetizer, not your Uncle Howard.

Ingredients
1 package of cherry tomatoes
olive oil
cream cheese
fresh basil leaves
baguette

Directions
1. Preheat oven to 350°F.
2. Wash the cherry tomatoes and slice in half.
3. Place in a baking tray, drizzle with olive oil, and roast for 15 minutes.
4. Cut baguette into half-inch slices, and spread each generously with cream cheese.
5. Place a basil leaf on each slice.
6. Place a cut tomato on top of basil.
7. Put back in the oven for an additional 10 to 15 minutes.
8. Serve and gloat.

Smoked Salmon, Fennel, and Goat Cheese Toasts

This is great for grossing out the kids (Cheese? From a goat? Are you crazy, Mom?) which ensures that all of the adults will get to eat some. The recipe was originally written with this accompanying piece of advice: "Goes perfectly with champagne." I find this to be particularly true if you drink the champagne *while* you are making it.

Ingredients

8 oz soft, fresh goat cheese
1 1/2 tbsp chopped fresh tarragon
1 tbsp fennel seeds, finely crushed with the bottom of a pan or a hammer
2 tsp grated lemon peel
1/2 tsp coarsely ground black pepper
2 1/2 tbsp olive oil
30 thin slices baguette
12 oz thinly sliced smoked salmon
lemon peel strips (for garnish)

Directions

1. Preheat oven to 350°F. Mix first five ingredients in a small bowl. Set aside. Have a drink.
2. Brush oil over both sides of each piece of bread. Place slices on large baking sheet. Bake five minutes, flip over, and bake five more. Have another sip.
3. Spread cheese mixture on toasted bread, top with salmon, and garnish with lemon peel.

4. Serve and impress (if you're not too drunk and can manage
    not to drop the tray on the way to the living room, that is).

Show Me the Red Meat!

I love barbecued steak. I don't, however, love barbecuing in the winter. It's cold in Canada! Yes, even Toronto is cold, you Prairie doubters. So, if you're like me and can't stand the thought of digging a path to the BBQ in your snow-covered backyard, try this stove-top recipe. Try not to think about the fried-in-the-pan steaks your mom used to make in the '70s. This is good.

Ingredients
3 garlic cloves
8 tbsp unsalted butter, softened
1 tsp dried thyme
black pepper
salt
2 tbsp vegetable oil
4 steaks (any type will do, but rib-eyes are lovely)

Directions
1. Chop garlic finely and sprinkle with salt. Continue to chop until mashed into a paste. Gaze out into your backyard and flip your BBQ the bird.
2. Put the garlic paste, butter, thyme, and a pinch of pepper into a bowl and beat in the softened butter. Ask your husband what he's doing with all of his spare time since he's not firing up the BBQ.
3. Melt half the butter mixture in a small saucepan over medium heat. Save the rest for a great garlic base for your mussels (see next recipe). Tell husband to set the table. What else is he doing?

4. Heat the oven to 425°F.

5. Heat the vegetable oil over high heat for about two minutes, or until very hot. Season the steaks with salt and pepper to taste. Add them to the pan and brown them well on one side, about five minutes. Flip them and brush liberally with the melted garlic butter. Finish cooking in the oven (to desired finish), and keep spreading the butter (you can add in a workout next week).

6. Remove the steaks from the oven. Remember, like men, they need a good rest before they're any good to you. Let stand at least five minutes before serving.

7. Spoon any remaining juice from the pan onto the meat.

8. Have husband clear the table afterward.

Flex Your Mussels

Mussels are an awesome and impressive appetizer or main course to serve at family gatherings. First of all, they're cheap— really—and second, they seem fancy and fussy but nothing could be further from the truth. Here's an easy recipe I got from a real Maritimer; it never fails.

Ingredients
Mussels—plan for about half a pound per person (this recipe is for 3 to 5 pounds of mussels)
one large onion, diced
1 tbsp butter
minced garlic, to taste
1 cup water
1 cup white wine

Directions
1. Keep mussels refrigerated right until you use them, but don't let them sit in your fridge for more than 12 hours. They stink. Trust me.
2. Scrub the shells in cold water, carefully removing any dirt/strands.
3. In a *large* pot (the biggest one you have), sauté the onion in the butter until transparent. (The onion, not the butter.) Then add the garlic, and sauté for 30 seconds, being careful not to let it brown.
4. Pour in the water and white wine, and bring the whole mess to a boil.

5. Pour the mussels into the pot, cover, and boil for 5 to 10 minutes.

6. Pour mussels and broth into a large bowl, or bowls, and serve. (Note: mussels that aren't open died before you could cook them. *These are bad. Don't pry them open and eat them.*)

7. Serve with baguette to mop up the broth. Awesome.

8. Remember to take the empty mussel shells out to the garbage that night. Don't clean them and don't let your kids play with them. They have sharp edges and a tendency to, well, stink if not cleaned properly. Learn from my experience.

Once 'Round the Kitchen Cupboards

If it's cheap, and it tastes good, you win. I tried this recipe on a visiting family with *seven* children (including triplets!), all in their teen years. These people are big eaters who we needed to feed (in addition to our own family of *six*) and simultaneously impress. Not sure if we impressed, but this is a great way to take any cut of meat and make it taste like the best cut of meat. Contrary to the old English expression "any meat is good meat if you boil it long enough," I believe that "any meat is good meat if you marinate it long enough in enough different ingredients." Start at one end of the kitchen cupboard system and work your way around until you have everything lined up.

Ingredients
1 cup red wine
1 cup white vinegar
1 / 2 cup cooking oil
1 / 2 cup finely chopped onion
4 tbsp sugar
2 tbsp Worcestershire sauce
2 tsp dry mustard
1 / 2 tsp pepper
1 / 2 tsp chili powder
1 / 2 tsp dried thyme
4 cloves fresh garlic
dash of hot pepper sauce
5 to 6 lb boned and rolled cross rib roast. (You will likely have to ask your butcher to prepare this for you. I once asked my local

grocery meat counter for this and they said, "we don't *do* cross rib roast." Give me a break. I don't *do* that store anymore.)

Directions

1. Combine all ingredients, except your cheap cut of beef.
2. Place beef into a resealable bag and pour the marinade over it.
3. Close bag securely and marinate overnight in the fridge, or better still, two nights. Turn the meat several times.
4. Heat barbecue to medium.
5. Reserving marinade, remove meat and place on rotisserie. Place a drip pan with half an inch of water underneath the roast, over the coals.
6. Barbecue on the rotisserie for 1 1/2 to 2 hours, basting with marinade for last 30 minutes. Use a meat thermometer to cook to desired done-ness.
7. Heat remaining marinade on the stove or in the microwave and serve as sauce with roast.
8. Carve meat. Serve alone, or in buns. Cheap and cheerful.

10
Children and Others Like Them
Food, Friends, and Fun. Not.

"Teenagers are particularly anxious to have their friends find their parents well-groomed and gay, and their home attractive. They want so intensely to be proud of their surroundings and people. For the high school boy or girl, social success is a stimulus to scholastic success. You can be of most help by being understanding and cooperative."
—Blanche Hall, *The Art of Entertaining*, 1952

"Hadn't heard that having gay parents could increase your social standing, but hey, I'm open-minded. Actually, my discovery is that what teenagers most want out of their parents is their absence. Buy the food, stuff it in a cupboard in the basement, and tell them to get lost. You'll both be happy."
—Kathy Buckworth, 2010

"Occasionally son or daughter may wish to entertain, but hesitate to bring their young friends home to dinner, thinking it will be too much for mother or that it will infringe on father's right to quiet."
—Hall, 1952

"Are you frigging kidding me? Children don't actually care what is 'too much for mother,' and since when did a father have a right to have quiet?"
—Buckworth, 2010

With two teenagers in the house, it's not unusual for me to come home and find a few backsides peeking out from the open door of my fridge—some I recognize and some I don't. Mine or not, the owners of these backsides have a lot in common—namely a raiding instinct when it comes to my kitchen. What's more, they seem to enjoy this hunt-and-forage system.

If I should ever do anything overly motherly, like prepare a "snack tray" (normally done when I have friends of my own coming over and am looking for a way to keep said teenagers basement-bound while we drink wine in the living room), I can guarantee you that it will scarcely be picked at when I go down hours later to pick it up. It seems like eating is no different from other kid-centric activities: it's just not as much fun when your parents give you permission to do it—particularly during the teen years.

When kids are younger—like my 7- and 10-year-old—they and their rascally friends are always on the lookout for "snacks." In Chapter 5, we firmly established the fact that we have produced a generation of snack eaters—children who can't go longer than half an hour during a sporting activity, or ten minutes at an outdoor park, without asking "what's for snack?" So, like obliging sherpas, we parents carry these snacks *everywhere*. At the same time, we're expected to have an endless supply of snacks in our kitchen cupboards. And, for the record, a real "snack" cannot be fruit. That's just too much work for me.

Birthday Madness

But wait, there's more! Clearly, handling the day-to-day demands of your snacking children and their hungry hangers-on isn't enough to keep moms occupied and challenged. Nope—once or twice a year (or four times, if *you're insane*), you have to tackle the madness associated with a birthday party.

Birthday parties are the extreme version of having children over to your house. Thanks to the hype surrounding the event, the theme and the food, the expectations are almost never met. Not theirs, or yours. And with four children (I told you—insane), it seems that at any point during the calendar year I'm planning a child's birthday party, running late trying to book a venue for a child's birthday party, or standing in line at the dollar store waiting to pay for a cart full of crap that will make up a Hefty-sized loot bag for a party. Putting aside all of these logistics, however, the core of most children's parties is, of course, the food. (Did you *read* the title of the book before you bought it?)

My memory may be deceiving me (and, frankly, I sort of like it when it does that), but when I was a kid going to birthday parties in the '60s and '70s, not only were we dressed to the nines, but the only food on offer was, well, birthday cake. There may have been a smattering of tiny sandwiches and the occasional sorry-looking jellied salad, but basically that was it. And the sandwiches were most likely peanut butter on white, made by my mother's hand ten minutes before the guests arrived.

Today, no matter what time of day or night the party is held (2:00–5:00 seems to be a very popular and annoying time of day at which to do these things), the kids arrive home stuffed to the gills with junk food, just as you're starting to prepare your own dinner. Throws them off for days. Not only is there not a peanut butter sandwich in sight, one seems to be absolutely required to serve pizza. Not pizza you can buy for $4.99 and put in the oven yourself, mind you, but pizza that arrives squealing up your driveway in a Pinto, encased in a bright orange cardboard box. "Party size," I believe they call it. A kid's birthday party without pizza is an anomaly. You might get one where Mom goes crazy and cracks out the KFC, but I certainly can't recall a small-sandwich buffet—except for the one time my tomboy daughter was invited to a Princess's Tea Party that took place at what I'm pretty sure was once a brothel. And the tiny designer sandwiches were most definitely not made by the overcoiffed mom who ran around making sure the girls' tiaras were on just so for the group picture.

So you have the pizza (and there's always one kid scraping off the sauce, right onto your carpet). You might even have thrown onto the table a bag of those tasteless mini-carrots (to appease the one or two hovering parents who can't trust you to watch their 8-year-old for two hours). Done? Oh *no*, my friend. You have to deal with the cake. And it can't be just *any* cake. It's got to be peanut-free, wheat-free, gluten-free (okay, I admit it; I have no frickin' clue what a gluten is), egg-free, dairy-free—you may as well just serve them up a piece of cardboard that you've decorated with a painting of SpongeBob. Honestly, it wouldn't matter if you did. I have discovered that birthday cake is purely for decoration and for the mouths of the fat dads who come to pick up their kids. Yes, startling revelation here: most kids don't actually like or eat birthday cake. Those who do deign to dive in will eat all of the icing—with their fingers—and leave hunks of cake all over the table and floor. Save yourself some trouble and skip it. Show them a picture.

I know it's polite and safe to ask parents if their children have any allergies before having them to your house for a party, but let's all agree to make sure only relevant allergies are discussed. Peanuts? Sure. Dairy? Absolutely. Yellow jackets and polyester? Since we're going to be stuck in the party room of the local bowling alley for a good two hours, I'm pretty sure I can avoid a huge swarm of killer bees while your child is in my care. As for the polyester...well, we'll just hope that the Seniors Bowling League doesn't wander in here by mistake looking for some hugs.

As an allergy aside, my youngest daughter has always had an itch somewhere, since the day she was born. Mostly she likes to itch the lower part of her body—including but not limited to her legs. In the interest of good hygiene and propriety, I took her to an allergist, who confirmed that she was in fact allergic to mould.

"Is that a comment on my housekeeping?" I asked, ready to assault him with the travails of the busy working mom of four.

"No. The good news is, it's an outdoor thing—plants, dirt, lawn, etc. The bad news is it's everywhere. Buy her some anti-histamine and anti-itch cream and get on with your lives."

So we did … and I've yet to warn another party-giving parent about the danger of Bridget being exposed to a mouldy house plant while playing hide-and-seek. I like to live dangerously that way. Mom will have enough to do trying to get the orange soda out of their light blue sofa.

Some Handy Snack Recipes

Now you've done it. You've invited some friends over who have (ugh) children, and guess what, they're going to be bringing them along. We have a couple of choices here. We can pretend that all we serve are healthy snacks (start cutting up those apples, peeling those carrots, and slicing those cucumbers! Quick—throw some granola on top as well!), or you can do what I do: zip over to the closest grocery or convenience store and load up on the "Family Mega-Sized" bags of potato chips, cheese crunchies, pork poopies (or whatever they're called), and give the kids what they *really* want. As an added bonus, this approach will keep them out of your hair for a good half an hour while they scarf down these forbidden fruits.

But, okay, let's say you actually do have a small Martha Stewart gene (not to be confused with small Martha Stewart jeans, because those would just be nasty) and you actually care about the opinion of the moms and maybe dads who are coming over to visit. Here are some quick, mostly healthy snack options.

Ants on a Log

Kids love this old standby. It's basically just pieces of cut celery, filled with peanut butter and topped with raisin "ants." But for the peanut-free crowd, you can use Cheeze Whiz with bits of bacon (yum—again with the bacon, I know), cream cheese with cheddar cheese grated on top, or even a bit of tuna salad and a resurrection of the raisin "ant" theme.

Nacho Chips, Kid-Style

Spread out some nacho chips, but go heavy on the tomatoes and lettuce on top, and lighter on the grated or melted cheese. You're *almost* tricking them into eating a salad. Throw some cucumber on there while you're at it.

Toasted Whatevers

Stock up on tiny packaged "Paris Toasts." For some reason these appeal to kids—*ooooh*, little toasts. You can spread anything on them—from jam and peanut butter to cream cheese, pâté, Nutella, and beyond. Kids love the idea of eating something miniature for some reason. Get them to do the spreading them-selves, and they're out of the way for an even longer period of time. Word to the wise—don't give them a sharp knife.

Part III
Take It Easy

"*The age of your children is a key factor in how quickly you are served in a restaurant. We once had a waiter in Canada who said, 'Could I get you your check?' and we answered, 'How about the menu first?'*"
—Erma Bombeck

11
Mom's Night Off
The Joys of Eating Out

"*You deserve a break today, so get up and get away, to McDonalds.*"
—McDonald's ad campaign (1971–75)

"*The only break you get from going out to eat is not having to take the blame for the crappy meal.*"
—Kathy Buckworth, Professor of Quiet Yelling in Public Studies

There are times, usually on a Friday night, when I just don't feel like making a family dinner. Okay, so I feel that way on most nights. It's just that, on a Friday night, for some reason, society allows me to consider the possibility of taking a night off from the kitchen. Heck, there's a whole restaurant chain named TGIF, so I can't be the first person to think this way, right?

As with most familial situations, the idea of taking my brood out to a restaurant—and in turn alleviating the need to cut, chop, cook, set, clear, and force a dinner down their throats—is more pleasant than the experience itself. No matter how many times I learn this lesson, I keep trying to change the outcome. Clearly, I am an idiot.

While it's true that a dinner out effectively eliminates the mechanical requirements of putting together a dinner and clearing it up afterward, I fail to realize (time and time again) a crucial difference between the restaurant dinner and the at-home dinner. At a restaurant, you spend a lot of (you guessed it) *time* waiting. Not only waiting, it turns out, but waiting *in front of your kids*. You don't do this at home. Try as I might, I can't really recall forcing my kids to sit at our kitchen table, speaking politely to each other and to me, while I prepare dinner. Yet, somehow, I expect that they can and will do this when we're at a restaurant. A real family restaurant would actually allow you to order before you arrived, so that the moment you sat down, dinner would immediately be shoved in front of the children. Just like at home. That's a real "Mom's Diner," as far as I'm concerned. Actually, to make this really authentic, there should be no "ordering." "Mom"—whomever she might be—decides what you're going to get and puts it in front of you, just like at home.

When I was a kid and parents rightfully ignored their children at home and in public, we used to go a pizza place with long wooden tables and benches, pitchers of pop and beer, and old silent black-and-white Laurel and Hardy movies on a projector screen. When I think about it, that was pretty state of the art. This was the '70s, after all. In Winnipeg. Anyway, we used to sit—entranced by the sight of the piano sliding down the stairs and crashing into a hapless Stan, munching away on our pizza—

while Mom and Dad visited with neighbours, had a few drinks, and occasionally threatened to smack us or send us to the car. Ah, the good old days. No kids' menus, just half portions and all the pop you could drink. (Because it was the only pop you were allowed all week, and that pitcher was likely the same size as a regular Big Gulp is today.)

So there we were in Shakey's Pizza on Portage Avenue in Winnipeg, when my Mom decided to enter a draw for the "World's Largest Pizza." (I guess the truth in advertising standards weren't quite as high in those days as they are today.) And we won! In fact, this pizza was so large that we had to go to a different Shakey's to get it—one with world's largest pizza oven, one imagines. The thought of consuming all that pizza (the world's largest, did I mention?) scared my folks so much that they invited along another family of six, and between us (okay, mostly between my sister and one of their boys), we demolished the entire thing. And this was real pizza—the type with just cheese, sauce, and meat. Not the crumbled goat cheese, chicken pesto, organic sun-dried-tomato type you get today. Or, on the other end of the new pizza spectrum, the type that comes with the crust stuffed with cheese, double deep-fried, or supersized. Because goodness knows we're not all quite fat enough yet.

Small Talk and Other Coping Mechanisms

Back in the present day—where a parent's main job, it seems, is to offer non-stop entertainment—it's worth remembering that children normally fight because they're bored. And what better place to get bored than at a crowded steakhouse on a Friday night, where you're being forced to sit unnaturally close to your stinking siblings *and* make conversation with your parents about school, of all things. Dads are particularly bad at small talk (well, men in general are bad at small talk, and let's just say that becoming a Dad doesn't improve this talent). Here's an example from my personal stash:

Dad: So, how's school, Alex?

Alex: Fine.

Dad: So, how's school, Bridget?

Bridget: Today at recess I saw a dead rat.

Dad: So, how's school, Nicholas?

Nicholas: Where was the rat, Bridget? I didn't see it. You're making it up.

Dad: So how's school, Victoria?

Victoria: How do you think?

Bridget: There was too a rat. Its head was split in half.

Dad: Where's the waiter?

Me: You really have nothing else left in that witty conversation arsenal of yours, do you?

Dad: What? The kids don't want to talk to me. I tried.

So, you've exhausted the small-talk option for killing time. What next? Sorry to break this to you, but unless your kids are under four and enjoy colouring on the tablecloth, you're sort of out of options. You can't even lube up the kids with a quick cocktail, as you can with adults when you decide to go out for dinner. Here's a tip: forget ordering the Shirley Temple; it's basically coloured 7UP priced at $6.95. The kids either won't drink it or they'll find a way to spill it right inside your purse.

Despite the challenges, we do occasionally take our kids out to a restaurant where you don't have to line up and hold a tray (more on those in a minute), usually a garden-variety chain such as Kelsey's, Montana's, etc. On purely personal grounds, I refuse to go to a restaurant whose name includes the words "Nasty," "Filthy," or "Crabby." We can get that at home, thanks very much. Anyway, ours are the types of restaurants where some insanely perky gal or guy will come over and demonstrate their excellent upside-down writing skills as they both say and inscribe their equally perky name on your paper tablecloth. Here's the thing, though: I really don't care what your name is—just bring me the wine list and some crayons before I totally lose it, okay?

Once the kids have decided on their kids' menu item choice, and I've ordered a litre of house white with one glass, we can take in the restaurant's folksy outdoor motif, marvel at the moosehead on the wall, and stare with envy at the child-free couples sitting at the adjoining bar. They really shouldn't let us see them, or maybe we just shouldn't look. There are, after all, plenty of distractions, what with pulling apart warring children, knocking over 20 ounce cups of Coke, and visiting the bathroom a record 11 times during the course of one meal. By the time the bill comes, I'm literally chugging the last of my wine, and both my husband and I are vowing never to take these animals out in public again. Good times.

I've learned not to take my children to restaurants with any sort of ethnic leaning. Their opening remarks—always within earshot of the waitstaff, of course—are often insulting, inappropriate, and embarrassing (sort of like the things *you* said when you met his in-laws for the first time). The one exception to this rule might be that ubiquitous "Chinese" restaurant, The

Mandarin, whose buffet contains such exotic Chinese delights as French fries, mac and cheese, and, of course, Buffalo wings. Bear in mind that I grew up in a house where my English-born-and-raised Mom thought that spaghetti and meatballs was a delightfully foreign dish. She would open the can of Catelli tomato sauce and then proceed to cut it with Campbell's Cream of Tomato soup because she thought it would be too spicy otherwise. It probably would have been, as well. My husband's upbringing was much the same. At one family get-together, I made an enormous Crock-Pot full of chili. My mother-in-law took one bite, looked at me and said "I think you put chili powder in this chili, didn't you, Kathy?" Because I'm sneaky like that, I said "Yes. Don't you?"

"Oh no, that would make it much too spicy for us."

Despite some early and unsuccessful efforts to buck the trend (I may never, more's the pity, eat Indian food again), my children have grown up with this same nervous palate. The exception is my teenage son, who puts hot sauce on everything—sort of the adolescent ketchup, I suppose). The result is that most of the time we go out it's not very exciting. It's loud, people argue, the food isn't all that good, and the wine is cheap. Just like at home.

Faster Is Not Necessarily Better

If a "real" restaurant experience—complete with waiting time and other challenges—can be a bit of a trial, eating out in *fast-food* restaurants is something that all children love. In fact, it wasn't until I reached my early 40s that I realized that most fast food is actually quite horrible. Sure, it's terrific for the grease factor one requires when suffering a hangover, but other than that, not so much.

I've attempted to share this hard-earned knowledge with my offspring, to no avail. Two of my kids have recently discovered Wendy's latest invention, The Baconator. As a former marketer, I absolutely love the name. Well done, branding department. From a mom standpoint, however, it's another story. This double-burgered bacon monstrosity has 830 calories, and a full 51 grams of fat. Basically, if you have one of these for lunch, you needn't eat for another three days—an approach I've discovered kids are generally not good at sticking to, never mind the adults. In fact, the least calorie-laden dish on the Wendy's menu is the hamburger in the kid's meal, which comes in at 220. This calorie count, of course, doesn't include fries, drinks, etc. We all know this, right? And FYI, it is not "illegal" to order the kids' meal if you're not a kid anymore. I do it all the time. And I'm an old lady.

I don't mind getting my kids fast food—not at all. It's generally cheap and normally can be eaten in a van without too much spillage—primary requirements when dealing with a full hockey or soccer calendar and four kids. On the "con" side, the most damaging part of the fast-food revolution is that kids now have an expectation that we can get their meals for them just as fast at home. My own kids have a hard time waiting for the Kraft Dinner to cook (nine minutes, just so you know). Of course, the fastest food they could eat at home is the aforementioned leftover. What I need to do is invest in some fast-food wrappers, place the leftover lasagne inside a bun, and wrap it up. The McPasta. Whadda you think?

Fun with Grown-ups

As I mentioned at the start of this book, not all bad/weird/annoying food situations come when your children are sitting in front of you. I mostly enjoy eating out with friends, particularly if we've all made the sensible decision to leave our children at home. I say mostly because there have been a few times when I've thought to myself, really? You're an adult and you behave like that in public? One such occasion was with a colleague I was meeting. I arrived at the restaurant about ten minutes early, and to my surprise she jumped up from a table, having arrived early herself. So early, in fact, that she had already ordered her lunch, received it, and was halfway through eating it.

Now, I know I'm possibly not the best company in the world and there are certainly some people who would like to keep their interactions with me to a minimum, but I found this a bit rude. I ordered soup (the fastest thing on any menu) and tried to finish it before she could finish her salad. I was worried that this was all an elaborate attempt to stick me with the bill. Okay, no I wasn't; I just found it to be a little weird but kind of funny and I'd like to try it out on someone else just to see their reaction. Send me an invite.

With regards to sticking someone with the bill, however, we all know at least one friend who will consume a few glasses of wine, order an appetizer, and then insist that because they didn't have as much as everyone else we all should tally up at our own items on the bill, and not just divide it evenly. Then they will proceed to leave only half of what they owe because they don't consider tax and tip to be their responsibility. The only way to break these people of this habit is to call them on it, or do the math for them. Of course, if they're really that cheap, they'll say "Oh, maybe you can spot me $20," and then never pay you back. Make a mental calculation before agreeing to dine out with one of these people. The price tag is a bit steep, so if their company is not up to snuff, go ahead and exclude them from the next outing.

I always overpay. I figure it makes up for the fact that I can't be bothered to deliver on the sparkling company and conversation side of the equation. Aside from paying up, there are some other handy rules for adults wishing to dine out with success:

1. Please arrive on time, or even early, particularly if you're meeting only one other friend. If you're late, the wait staff will give that one on-time person the evil eye (especially in a crowded lunch spot where time is limited for table turnaround), and you will subsequently have bad service (for which you will overtip, because you feel guilty). This will, however, give you something new to complain about, and let's face it, if you're the type of person to leave a friend sitting alone for 20 minutes in a busy restaurant, you're arrogant anyway and you'll have a million other complaints to file before the day is out. Phew.

2. If your time for the meal is limited, state that at the beginning so you and your companions can pace your meals. You won't leave someone else with a half-eaten meal or the bill. This is both embarrassing and cheap.

3. Don't be rude to the waiter or waitress. PLEASE. Most of us parents are so thrilled to be out for the evening, away from

the extremely rude behaviour of our children, that we honestly don't mind a little attitude from the teen server. PLUS, many of us have teenagers. We know that talking instead of scowling takes a huge amount of effort. Hell, surly Josh or Jessica should be commended for making progress. Oh, and many of us worked in restaurants in our own youth. We know precisely what disgusting things can be done to a meal behind closed doors.

4. Don't ask to switch tables more than once.

5. Unless it is completely raw (and shouldn't be), or burned (and shouldn't be), or arrives with a dead cockroach on top of it, please don't send food back to the kitchen. If it's "not what you thought it would be," that's your tough luck. A short note to the restaurant on improving their menu descriptions will suffice.

6. Meg Ryan was cute in *When Harry Met Sally* with all of those substitutions and dressings on the side. You're not Meg Ryan. (Either is she anymore, actually). You're not cute. Keep your special requests to a minimum. It's a real turnoff to your fellow diners.

These may sound like fairly severe rules just for the pleasure of eating out in my company, and maybe they are. But I only get to do this once in a while—to eat in a restaurant that doesn't feature an indoor playground, I mean—and I'll be damned if I'm going to let you folks annoy me as much as my regular dining companions. Now sit down and put your napkin on your lap. Can I cut up that meat for you?

12
Easy Does It
Drive Thru, Squeeze Bottles, and Other Conveniences

"Of course you're a busy lady. That's why we have our section of jiffy meals that rival the kind that take hours to prepare. You get a head start with packaged, canned, and frozen foods."
—Better Homes & Gardens New Cook Book (1965)

"Skip the head start and go right to the finish line. What, you're too good for takeout pizza once in a while?"
—Kathy Buckworth (getting over herself, 2010)

The world we live in is nothing less than "convenient." Or so the marketers and new product developers would have us believe. Who needs to cook in their own kitchen? With prepacked, frozen, ready-to-serve, just-add-water meals abundant in our grocery stores, and the huge array of fast-food restaurants we drive past on our way home from work, the hockey arena and, well basically anywhere that's more than two blocks from our house, there's really no need to invest in a good set of pots and pans, or dishes for that matter. What, you think you can cook better than a Colonel, a King, or a Jack in the Box? Guess again— that is, if you're asking your kids about who might win.

The only problem with "convenience" foods is that they introduce other elements which aren't so convenient. Like the fact that you're going to have to move up a pant size every month.

We all know this, but the appeal of fast and easy is something not just reserved for horny high school boys. The Great Marketers know this, so they have developed "in-home" convenient solutions to pesky meal preparation, such as anything that can go into a squeezy bottle shall and will go into a squeezy bottle. I support this innovation. It makes my kitchen a more pleasant and convenient place to be.

On the other hand, you've got the intimate setting of the front seat of your messy and child-laden car, with you yelling into a broken speaker to a texting teenager absolutely intent on putting *extra* onions on that burger instead of eliminating them. Why do we have this love affair with the drive-thru? Can we somehow blame this on the men because it has to do with food *and* cars?

Part of the appeal of the drive-thru window for kids is the implication that they are going to be able to eat their meal somewhere other than the boring old kitchen or dining room table. If you have active kids enrolled in many time-consuming and inappropriately scheduled sports, chances are good that they will be eating more than a few meals in the family vehicle. There are some pros and cons to this arrangement. Allow me, if you will:

Drive-Thru Pros

- Because the kids are secured in their seats, there is little opportunity for the kicking that usually goes on at the dinner table. Their hands should be full of some fatty, greasy burger and/or fries, thus rendering them unable to pinch, poke, or flip off a nearby sibling. Imagine if you could get this type of limb control at home.

- If you say there's no ketchup, there ain't no ketchup, baby. You've just pulled away from the drive-thru, you're running ten minutes late for *their* game, and it's not like you have a cupboard in your van. Let me rephrase that: You'd better *not* have a condiment cupboard in your van.

- If they don't like what they ordered, too flippin' bad. You can't just whip them up a PB and J. They can shut up and eat (hey, that's a great theme for a book, eh?).

- No pots and pans to clean up, no fighting over who clears the table, and no fighting over who gets the last Fudgsicle. (Funny, I don't really know anyone who orders dessert to go at these fast food places, do you?)

- For adults, the drive-thru can be used as a method of calorie control. Look, you ordered the garden salad, and it's all you have. Unless a kid decides to gift you his entire order of french fries, you may just stick to that low-carb diet, despite yourself.

Drive-Thru Cons

- If some idiotic server throws a packet of ketchup in with your order, the kids will believe it is their right to use it in the car. Even if your car has beige cloth seats. If it's a single packet of ketchup, there will be a huge fight, as an added bonus.

- About 50% of the time, your order will be wrong, and the child whose order is missing or contains an unwanted pickle will be traumatized until you can get to the arena and order them something disgusting there to make up for it.
- Your vehicle will stink like that meal for at least three days. Three weeks if you forget to remove the wrappers, which always contain the last bite of meat. And the abandoned pickle.
- If purchasing a children's meal, you are going to have to decide whether to order a "girl toy" or a "boy toy." Besides the sexist stereotyping that the squeaky voiced 15-year-old on the other end of the speaker doesn't want to know about, you're always going to choose wrong. If you get two of the same toys, they instantly lose their cachet (no one can brag that they got the better toy). If you get different toys, well you're stuck with the bragging, the fighting, and the "Mom! It's not fair!"—which always ends with, "I'm never doing this again!" That last part was you, from the front seat, and it's a lie, and you—and they—know it.
- The carbonated beverages that they serve with a "combo meal" (one of the world's most evil marketing inventions, by the way) are the size of a fire bucket. Each child will not only get hopped up on all the sugar in one of these babies, they will need to do a liquid readjustment within about 10 minutes of drinking one. This is not a good scenario inside an enclosed space— picture with me, if you will, a 4-year-old straining against his carseat, flailing wildly about, as his newly trained bladder reacts in shock and distress to this unsettling environment.

- One kid will inevitably leave his/her fries and you will inevitably eat them. Without ketchup, because you don't allow it in the van. And you may as well drink that leftover pop, too. Where's the closest washroom?

Generally, I've found that dads don't see any downside to the in-vehicle eating, unless they're worried about stains on the seats, or having the greasy oil smell overtake their coveted new car smell. Note the theme here? His concerns are not about the food, or even the kids. It's all about the car.

While I will admit to succumbing to the drive-thru circle of hell on more than one occasion, I am mostly able to avoid this meal aberration by reminding myself what an inglorious death it would be should I meet my demise upon the departure from the drive-thru lane. "Kathy Buckworth, 46, perished while attempting to "even out" the french fries in her children's Happy Meal bags, after she mistakenly pilfered too many of said fries from one bag, and not the other. An autopsy will be performed to confirm these results—although her unbuttoned jeans may suffice."

Road Trip!

Of course, fast food is not the only food you might have to serve in your car. On long road trips, many families choose to pack their own food. On the surface, this makes sense; after all, there's nothing like food from home—good, healthy, nutritious snacks that will keep the kids smiling and the waistlines trim. Now, many moms who subscribe to this notion are also under the mistaken impression that their clean, scrubbed, and happy kids will be singing camp songs in the car all the way to the Grand Canyon. Yes, that's right, I'm talking about *The Brady Bunch*. Not my family—or yours, for that matter.

Come to think of it, I'm not sure the Bradys took any food in the station wagon with them. You know, I'm not sure how they all fit in there either. I guess they had three in each row (don't forget Alice!) and maybe the dog as well. Was all of their luggage and camping gear in that garbage bag on top? We know one thing—it certainly didn't contain any food, because when they got to the campsite, the first job for the Brady men was to go fishing for dinner. Luckily, resourceful and sturdy Alice had snuck in a picnic basket (where the hell did you hide that in the car Alice—under your uniform?) with enough supplies to see nine hungry people through their week-long trip. It has always bothered me the way family eating was misrepresented on that show. So of course I was one of the first people to purchase *Alice's Brady Bunch Cookbook*, which contains such fantastic recipes such as "It's a Sunshine Day Scalloped Potatoes" and of course the "Grand Canyon or Bust Hiker's Mix." Cuz remember, the only thing the Brady boys caught during their fishing trip was Cindy! *Ha ha ha!* Phew.

The Buckworth Bunch

Yes, I know *The Brady Bunch* was a fictitious account of what a real family would actually be like. But, as I try to tell my real children, can't we just try to fake it once in a while? Particularly when we're out in public? Or in confined, moving spaces like the family vehicle?

Whether you're in a car or not, it's a universal truth that feeding children keeps them occupied. I like to start car trips with my children basically malnourished and starving. This way, I can drag out the process of feeding them teeny tiny bits of junk food over countless highway miles. At least that is the plan. I package up little resealable bags full of goldfish-shaped cheese crackers, my own homemade trail mix (okay, cereal and chocolate chips mixed together), some juice boxes and maybe even a fresh piece of fruit or two. This wholesome plan goes entirely out the window (sometimes literally) about five minutes into the drive when my husband makes an unscheduled, and frankly unapproved, stop at a local coffee shop. (Okay, he doesn't actually stop because we are a drive-thru nation.) As he barks out his order for strong coffee, the hapless attendant can't help but hear the call for donuts, muffins, bagels, and breakfast sandwiches that follow a barrage of yells, screams, and insults. Despite the drama, the procured "real" snacks keep everyone quiet until the same scene unfolds again at lunch, only to be replaced with the words *hamburger, nugget, super-size* and *gravy*.

By mid-afternoon, the car is full of paper wrappers and small cardboard containers, and the stench of grease hangs in the air. The only *good* thing to come out of this is that the kids are so bloated from their bad-food trip that they don't have the energy to poke each other. Very much. Goodnight, Alice.

The Squeezy Bottle and Other Kinds of Fun

As much as we adore our drive-thrus and road trips, our love of convenience when it comes to food-related items spreads far beyond the confines of the car. The food industry is awash with people trying to think up new and intriguing ways to save us time when it comes to preparing and eating food. They also keep trying to come up with new foods. I should point out that not all of these inventions have worked. My sister once tried to convince me that bacon-flavoured chocolate was a good idea. Now, while I love both bacon and chocolate, I have to say that the combination was not a success. Kind of like the Thrills gum from the '70s that tasted like soap. Actually, though, we all ate it all the time. Not sure why.

But there are some food inventions that, as a harried mom, I have totally embraced. Minced garlic in a jar? The best! Precooked bacon? We've already established that I love it. Lunchables? Sorry, but have to love these as well. There's something about someone else packaging up your kids' lunch that is just so satisfying.

I am also a fan of the recent trend of packaging cookies, crackers, and other snack foods into 100-calorie packages. Why? Because I can't be trusted not to eat the whole bag (plus, if I want, I can eat, like, eight of these and know I've still not hit the calorie level of a single Baconator. And that makes me feel good.)

The squeezy bottle trend is also one that I wholeheartedly embrace. In fact, nothing annoys me more these days than going into a restaurant that has glass ketchup bottles. You know, the type that you have to stick your knife up or whack away at the bottom of, looking like a red-faced demented maniac, only to have the ketchup shoot out across the table at an unsuspecting child, or worse, on your own white pants. I love squeezy mayonnaise, relish, mustard, steak sauce—it's all good. But I do have a few suggestions for other food items that would benefit from this packaging. Manufacturers, please pay attention.

- Peanut butter. In fact, why not peanut butter, and jam, *in the same tube*. Save on knives, spoons, and messy counter spills. Smart, right?
- Cheez Whiz. Such a natural. I'm a big fan of the American cheese in a can phenomenon—come on, Canada, get your Whiz in a tube.
- Pâté. Seriously. Terrific for picnics and a hit of liver when you need it most.
- Salted butter, for direct application onto individual pieces of popcorn.
- Sour cream and onion dip, for direct application on to individual potato chips. (Come on, you like this one, don't you?)
- Canned pasta. Straight into the kid's mouth in the van—no stopping in between lessons and no messy thermos cleanup. Maybe mini-mini-ravioli as well.

Besides the squeezy bottle, there are likely many things that food manufacturers and packagers could do to help both us and the environment. For instance, why is it that for years only ice cream was served in an edible container? Thanks to the taco salad bowl, bread bowl, and dip bowl people, we can now consume even more stuff when we sit down for a meal. Because goodness knows we North Americans haven't been eating nearly enough lately.

Who Knew? State Fair Secrets

Of course, some of the world's weirdest food inventions have nothing to do with edible bowls or squeezy bottles. They don't even come from the French, with their predilection for things such as horse, goose livers, and other disgusting internal organs of animals, or from the Eastern European countries with their love of all things pickled. Believe it or not, some of the strangest food inventions of all have come from the United States—a nation dedicated to finding new and innovative ways to get fatter, quicker. And where do most of these foods come from? Not the corporate offices of the ubiquitous fast-food restaurant chains, nor the upscale eateries found in New York City and San Francisco. Nope, these beauties come from the heartland of the nation—the State Fair.

Here's a recent sampling of the most popular menu items at US State Fairs. My thanks to www.delish.com for unearthing these creations.

Chicken-fried bacon. Now, don't get me wrong. As I have confessed in previous chapters, I think bacon is great with just about anything (with the possible exception of horse—sorry, Pierre). But I honestly don't know what "chicken fried" means. I've heard of "chicken-fried" steak, but, like Jessica Simpson and her tuna/Chicken of the Sea misunderstanding, I'm not really sure how a chicken gets involved in the process. Whatever it is, you can bet it's guaranteed to drive up your cholesterol and waist size.

Pizza in a cone. This is just pure marketing genius. In a world dedicated to eating on the go, this makes perfect sense. Pizza is already a hand-held food—beware of those who eat pizza with a knife and fork—but cut it the right way and twist it into a cone shape, with the crust side exposed, and—voila!—it's even easier to shove into your yap! And let's face it—anything in a cone sounds good. Update: This just in. Some fiendish inventors have just produced the Bacon Cone. I'm hyperventilating.

Hot Steak Sundae. When I first mentioned this one to my husband he said "Well, that sounds disgusting." Not so fast, Mr. Big Meat Eater. While the word "sundae" may imply an ice cream confection of sorts, in this case it's simply a visual aid. Picture strips of beef layered in a bowl, topped with mashed potatoes, and served with a generous dollop of gravy on top. Sprinkle with high-fat cheddar cheese and, if you really want to make it look like a traditional sundae, throw a cherry tomato on top. Be forewarned, though that the cherry is *not* deep-fried and might accidentally work toward getting something nutritious and non-fattening into your system (sorry about that.) It's a meal in a bowl (sort of like a party in a bag, but better). Sure, now you're drooling aren't you? The more calories and fat we can pack into a convenient serving container, the faster we can eat and move on to the next thing. Awesome! Wondering if that bowl comes in waffle...

Krispy Kreme Chicken Sandwich. Okay, go ahead, husband, you can find this one disgusting. It's exactly as it sounds. Slice a Krispy Kreme donut in half and slide a piece of fried chicken in it. Oh wait—put a slice of cheese in there, too. Wait! There's more! Serve with honey dressing. There. Eat your fattening dinner and dessert all at once. Hell, you saved enough time to have two.

Fried Avocado Bites. Had you at fried, didn't I? Take something reasonably healthy, (if calorie-rich), bread it, and fry it. Have three. No, four. Dip it in some mayo for the full experience.

Spaghetti and Meatball on a Stick. Yes, the country that brought you things in a cone also likes to bring you things on a stick. But this isn't just a simple meatball wrapped up in a big wad of spaghetti, or vice versa. No, *this* sucker is meat mixed with spaghetti into a ball, dipped in a batter, and deep-fried. Had you worried that this would be something *not* deep-fried, didn't I? Come on. Amateurs.

Fried Frog Legs. Okay, the French were the first to introduce frogs legs to mainstream cuisine, but you'd find them sautéed with a bit of butter, garlic, and onion. *C'est magnifique*. Not in the good ol' US of A. What do they do? Let me hear ya—yep, let's deep-fry those little things. Tastes like chicken. Fried chicken, that is.

Deep-fried Twinkies. Enough said.

Fried Coca-Cola. Hmmm. Let's ponder this one for a second. I'm already getting a good healthy dose of sugar and caffeine from the pop, but it's not quite enough. I need to add some . . . some . . . batter! Fried Coke is Coca-Cola-flavoured batter that's been deep-fried and finished up with Coca-Cola syrup, whipped cream, and cinnamon sugar. You sure we can't fit a piece of chicken in there somewhere?

Key Lime on a Stick. I do find it ironic that a country in which almost 30% of the population is obese keeps inventing food on a stick. You're not sticks, people, and food on a stick is *not* natural. Anyway, take a piece of already fattening key lime pie, put a stick in it, and dip it in melted chocolate. You can hold one of these in one hand, and a deep-fried meatball in the other. Perfect.

All this taking out and squeezing and deep-frying has to end somewhere—maybe in the apocalypse (hell, it may *cause* the apocalypse). I don't know how, and I don't know when, but I predict a backlash. With the increasing popularity of deep-fried turkeys—the preparation of which requires one to wear a full asbestos body suit—it's only a matter of time. While we're waiting for the End of Days, I say let's dip a whole cow. And put it on a really big stick.

13
An Inconvenient Truth
Diet Diaries, Jenny Craig, and Me

"Never eat more than you can lift."
—Miss Piggy

It is perhaps a little perverse to stick the dieting chapter right after the chapter in which we explored the pleasures of pizza in a cone and deep-fried Twinkies, but I like to torment myself. And why not? First, if we're going to talk about convenient food-related issues, why not throw some inconvenient ones into the mix as well? And it also sort of works with the basic dichotomy of my food-related life. I often feel like I spend most of my time trying to get my kids to eat something, while trying to get myself to stop eating everything. There is no mystery to losing weight and keeping it off. Eat less and exercise more. Emphasis on the *eat less*. Nothing is more disheartening than using a piece of equipment at the gym that calculates the exact number of calories you're burning. You realize that the 30 minutes of sweat equity you just put in equals exactly one granola bar—which you already ate because you thought you were being "good." I diet to take off the weight I've already put on, and I exercise to allow me to eat something good in the future. Yes, I'm the woman at the back of the weight class, muttering "one more glass of wine, one more glass of wine" as we heave and pump.

Dieting Tips. Cuz Lipo Sucks. Really.

A ripped personal trainer at my gym once told me she only eats to fuel up, because honestly, she doesn't really enjoy eating. It's just something she has to do. Seriously. Who is this freak? Someone who works out about a dozen times a week, and can't seem to enjoy the one main benefit of that excessive calorie burning—eating without thinking about every single spoonful that goes into your mouth. Ah, the perpetual dieter—i.e., most women. Show me a woman who doesn't think about how what she's eating will end up on her body and I'll show you a man. Or that one trainer, above. I've heard it said that fat people think about food all day long, except when they're eating it. And then they're just shoving it in their mouths and not really enjoying it. Dieters are like this, too. Successful or unsuccessful dieters, doesn't matter. Your whole day is spent thinking about the next 100 to 200 calorie snack you'll be consuming. When the blessed time arrives, you scarf it down as quickly as you can—and start planning the time and content of the next 100 to 200 calorie snack.

There are thousands and thousands of diets. The problem is that all of them have a sole objective: changing the way you eat right now. If you don't change the way you eat right now, you will continue to either gain weight or stay at the same weight. You *have* to change. But as the old joke about the psychiatrist and light bulb goes, it (you) has to really want to change. But change *and* diet at the same time? That's tough.

So what we really need to do is to discover a diet that doesn't require too much change, at least not all at the same time. And then—and here's the tricky part—we have to accept that we can't expect to see much of a change on the scale or in the tightness of our pants. At least not right away. To help get you started, I thought I'd share some tricks that have helped me with my own ongoing battle(s):

1. The pieces of mac and cheese, ends of cut-up hotdogs, and last bite of a hamburger bun left on your child's plate should never, ever be eaten by you. These things don't taste good, they are full of calories, and really, you don't want them. You just don't want to be bothered scraping the food off into the garbage, or you subconsciously feel as though you'll be wasting the food if you do this. No, you're not wasting it; you're avoiding applying it directly to your thighs. Make the right choice.

2. It is impossible to have one or two cocktail peanuts. Don't even start. Trust me on this one.

3. Like with the peanuts, for most of us, a wee glass of wine rarely sits alone in your stomach. It will be quickly joined by more of its ilk, as well as some nachos, dip, and a handful of those damn peanuts. Proceed with caution.

4. Cheese is a member of the dairy family. Eating to fulfil *Canada's Food Guide* is something all healthy eaters should do. *However*—that blue cheese and brie you're just about to inhale at the cocktail party would fulfil the dairy requirements for your entire block, for a week.

5. Tiny little Halloween chocolate bars (they seem to shrink every year) are not bad for you. Unless you eat 27 of them. That tends to add up.

6. Ignore the ads on television that say "reward yourself—you walked up the stairs at work today!" Yeah, you probably burned about 14 calories doing that, and the snack they're suggesting you reward yourself with is weighing in at about 80 calories a bite. You can do the math. You *need* to do the math.

7. Salad without dressing is excellent for you. Salad with oil and vinegar is still really good for you. Salad with any type of creamy dressing on it is in fact not salad anymore, it's lettuce coated in a rich, high-calorie sauce.

8. The muffins you buy from your local doughnut store are in fact cupcakes in disguise. Only bigger. Even calling them a cupcake is misleading; they're bigger than any cup you drink out of. They're a cake. Own it.

9. If you don't *order* the fries, you can't *eat* the fries.

I know it's hard to accept, but really, the only way in the world to lose weight is to stop eating so much. Really. So, when you think about it, the hardest work you're doing to lose weight is NOT doing something. NOT eating high-calorie foods, all the time. Going to the gym once a week is just not going to do it if you don't "break up with cheese," like Nia Vardalos did.

Spite and Revenge. Real Weight-Loss Tools

One of the main benefits of losing weight is often underplayed by the dieting and exercise industries. Oh sure, slimming down is good for your health, you can fit into those clothes you never thought you'd be able to wear, your spouse has a renewed interest in you (oh, yippee on that one, right girls?), and your kids are no longer embarrassed by you. (I seem to provide my children with a veritable warehouse of reasons to be embarrassed, so it's nice to eliminate one.) All of those things are great, but the real win on losing weight is the fact that you can flaunt it when you see your old friends. Spite and revenge are huge motivators for women, so I believe companies like Jenny Craig and Weight-Watchers could capture a much larger (*ha ha*) audience if they were to recognize this truth in some of their campaigns. I'll put my 20 years of marketing experience to use for them here:

"Lose the weight. Steal some husbands."
"Drop some pounds. And some friends."
"Look great in a swimsuit. Especially compared to *her*."
"Shhh, don't tell anyone you're dieting. Makes them even crazier."

I threw that last one in because it absolutely drives me *nuts* when I hear a twig like Cameron Diaz say that she wishes she had more curves, but she's just "built the way she is." What, um, perfectly? Shut up, Cameron, and eat something.

The Road to Svelte Is Paved with Food Interventions

So let's say you've decided you really do want to lose those extra pounds—not because Cameron Diaz is skinny, or because your best friend lost some weight, but because *you* want to. Good for you, girlfriend. I say go for it.

If you're like the vast majority of women who decide to undertake some sort of slimming-down regime, your first step may be to keep a food diary. Here's an example from one I started a few years ago. Read it and weep (for me):

Day 1

This is it. I've been talking about this for too long. Every day I weigh myself and every day, magically, my weight doesn't go down; instead, it creeps up. My pants are getting so tight I think I'm wearing thong underwear even when I'm not. The term *muffin top* isn't remotely cute and what I have more closely resembles a "mushroom top." Today I start.

Breakfast: Glass of skim milk, dry whole wheat toast, and four raspberries. Yum. This isn't so hard, I can do this. Next stop—the gym!

Wow, when they say Cardio Blast they mean it, eh? I'm exhausted. What do you mean that was just the warm-up. There's more? It gets harder? Crap. Plus, all the other women in this class are skinny already. Why are they here? If I looked like that, I'd be down in the cafeteria eating pancakes and bacon. I wonder when I'll ever have pancakes and bacon again—jumping jacks? Are you serious? I've had four kids, woman! Does it look like I have a Depends on under these skin-tight Lululemon pants? And who said

Lulus made your ass look small? Why are there so many mirrors in this room anyway? I can hardly breathe. Is it almost over? What does she mean, let's really get moving now?

Lunch: I may never walk again, but at least I made it through that workout. Reminder to self not to have bean burritos the night before any fitness class that includes extensive ab work. I'm pretty sure the women on either side didn't notice. Anyway, that's over and now I can focus on lunch. I'll just heat up one of these delicious-looking frozen entrees that guarantee I'll put only 280 calories in my mouth. Five minutes, okay. I can have a glass of water while I'm waiting. Whoa, just about blacked out there. Think I better eat something. Hmm. Carrots. Okay, now I see why you can eat a whole bag of carrots and not gain an ounce. After a while they taste like nothing and they don't fill you up at all. Where is that Orange Chicken with Multi-Grain Rice? *Ding*. Great! Looks good, smells good. Okay, I *think* it tasted good but the whole thing went down in about *three* spoonfuls. I'm still hungry. This will subside. The hunger is my weight loss. I can do this.

2:00: All diets recommend that you eat smaller meals during the day, so I think I'm entitled to a little snack here. Almonds are supposed to be really good for you. I'll just grab a little handful and that should do the trick. Okay, maybe two. Good enough.

4:00: I'm thinking about dinner. I'm so hungry I just licked the knife I used for my daughter's peanut butter sandwich, which I made for her lunch eight hours ago. Okay, more water, more diet pop. I can do this!

4:01: No, I can't.

4:02: Yes, I can.

4:03: I'm leaving the house. I can't stand looking at the food.

6:00: Dinner is on the table. Sure, look at that smug little bunch, digging into their spaghetti and meatballs, garlic bread, and salad. They look happy, don't they? I'm sure this salad and the feelings of joy that come from nurturing and feeding my family will more than make up for the fact that I'm not having what they're having. When I started this I promised I wouldn't make them suffer as a result.

6:25: Okay, when the ice cream came out, I lost it. Finish up alone, you selfish bastards.

6:30: I'm going to bed. There's no food in bed, and besides, I'm starting to feel something uncomfortable in my calves and my stomach. Must be a bit of a twinge from that class this morning. I'm sure a good night's sleep will work that out.

2 a.m.: Freaking starving. Stay in bed. Stay in bed. Stay in bed.

Day 2

Aaaargggh. I think I've pulled every single muscle in my body. I can't breathe without my stomach hurting, and I can't walk because my legs are seizing up. I can't lift my toothbrush or open my contact lens case, and the thought of squatting down to sit on the toilet? Well, I'll just hold it today, thanks. I can see that Depends are going to be a major part of this diet and fitness program. One thing I *can* do is get myself on this scale and see how much weight has fallen off me. I'm thinking two pounds at least. *Nothing?* I lost *nothing* and I'm starving and I feel like this? Are you *kidding* me? I must be getting my period.

I think I'll give my body a rest from fitness today—that's supposed to be good for you, plus I don't think I can get the extra-tight Lulu freaking shirt over my head this morning. I'll just focus on the food part today.

Breakfast: Okay, let's mix it up a bit this morning. I'm allowed 2/3 cup of this granola vegan-type cereal. Wow—good thing they only let you have a small amount because it tastes horrible and I'd never eat more of this sawdust than that. Surely it would be okay to add a banana just for flavour, right?

10:00: This time yesterday I was sweating it with the thin girls and I wasn't thinking about food, but now that I'm at home and I'm going with that smaller-meals-all-day theory, it's definitely time to have something. Hmm—a 100-calorie pack of granola bits. Well, that took 4.2 seconds to eat. More water I guess. Those seven diet colas just aren't doing the trick.

11:30: Close enough to lunchtime. Today? Frozen Oriental Ginger Beef Supreme. Five minutes. Okay, in you go. Today I think I'll have an entire container of cherry tomatoes while I wait. Well, *this* is pretty bland. I'm sure it wouldn't hurt to add just a little bit of salad dressing. I have to remember to get a low-calorie version of this blue cheese dressing. On the other hand, if I'm only having a little, I may as well have the real stuff. Four minutes and 30 seconds to go. Hmmm. Maybe just a couple of those garlic croutons as well.

2:00: That Ginger Beef was good, but it wasn't enough to keep a hamster alive. Those vegetables and dip worked so well earlier, I think I'll do some more of that. And this time I think I'll add some pita. How many calories could be in a flat piece of bread like that?

4:00: One chocolate bar. I've been good. I need a reward. Besides, I'm probably going to the gym again tomorrow. I'm a little stiff today, but not bad. Some people say it takes two days for the real soreness to set in but I don't think that will happen to me.

6:00: I had to make fried chicken tonight. The kids were counting on it, and it's our family tradition to have brownies on a Tuesday as well. My legs are really hurting now. I'm not sure there's an exercise class that works for me tomorrow.

8:00: Pass the chips, honey. Tomorrow? No, I don't have anything planned—sure, I can meet you for lunch. Let's go Greek! I'm pretty sure I'm PMSing. I'll start again next week.

Jenny, I've Got Your Number

Have you stopped laughing yet? Crying? Good. Now let me confess that after trying out that particular diet about 27 times in the past calendar year, I decided to go to the experts who had made Valerie Bertinelli look better than she'd looked in decades.

"Hello Jenny?"

Besides the failed attempts at dieting, I'll tell you what started all of this. It was the too-tight pants, the "muffin top" on my jeans that was threatening to become a whole loaf, *and* the old friend I saw who had always been about five pounds heavier than me—now inexplicably 20 pounds thinner. Add to that the fact that I had started to avoid looking at myself in the mirror at the gym (in those now horrible Lululemon pants I used to love). I'd also developed the habit of telling anyone who would listen that I looked fat on television only because the camera adds at least 10 pounds.

After a few months, this behaviour started to get a little alarming. So I called Jenny. I made arrangements to speak with a consultant, secure in the knowledge that I only had to lose 15 pounds to get me back to my goal weight of 120. I could easily do this by Christmas, I told myself. As I sat in the reception area waiting for my appointment, I almost felt guilty about taking up their time for such a small weight-loss program.

After speaking with a wonderful woman about why I wanted to lose weight (to beat those skinny bitches on my block, why else?), I went for my official weigh-in. I confidently took off my leather jacket, shoes, and heavy jewellery (hey, every ounce counts) and stepped on. Yikes; 147.8 pounds! No kidding! I think their scale is broken. Suddenly I have 27.8 pounds to lose. Well, *that* sucks. But they load me up with the prepackaged meals and away I go.

As the day goes on, I think about all of the times in the past six months when I thought I was looking really good but was actually quite fat. I am depressed by this, and I eat my last bowl of heavily buttered popcorn in preparation for the six long *months* it will likely take to lose this gargantuan amount of weight.

Funnily enough, I am psyched—seriously. I already work out two or three times a week so I don't have to change this routine, which would be even tougher. I'm psyched about the fact that, from this moment on, my pants are only going to get looser, not tighter. I'm a little worried about the fact that I'll be eating different meals than my family for dinner (breakfast and lunch are already isolated affairs), particularly in front of my overly picky teenage daughter, who would like to have something different from everyone every night. After all, I have repeatedly told her that we all eat the same thing (I'm not a short-order cook, yada yada yada). I'll figure out how to handle this, though. I'm good at spin.

I get through the first day pretty easily—I'm allowed all the coffee I can drink (my typing is getting faster and more frenzied by the minute), and vegetables are "free" as well, so I can keep going. There are points during the day when I feel hungry, but overall what I feel is in control. Dinner isn't an issue at all. The kids are eating early and are happy to see nuggets and fries on the table; they could care less if I'm eating or not. Interestingly, I think their nutritional intake will suffer as a result of my dieting, but I can't worry about all of us at once. If only I hadn't picked Halloween to start this. But I did. I don't mind not stealing candy out of the kids' bags; it's the wine drinking I do with the wandering neighbours that hurts the most. Ah well, as I once heard Elizabeth Hurley remark, "Most nights I go to bed hungry." Tonight will be one of those nights. Right now, 1200 calories doesn't taste like much.

As the diet went on, I faced some hard truths. For instance, the Jenny folk weren't wrong when they told me that the food was high in fibre. I also experienced some unexpected "ripple effects."

1. Higher grocery / drug store bills due to increased volume of toilet paper (see above).
2. Husband actually learning how to cook for himself—so far, Kraft Dinner, but it's a start.
3. Children loving me as I make all their favourites for dinner (which are naturally devoid of any nutritional value whatsoever).

The food is still pretty good, and I am drinking an inordinate amount of water, which has to be a good thing. Between that and the fibre—well, let's just say I'm getting a lot of reading done in a room traditionally reserved for my husband's print material.

I also like the "forced" snack time and I have to say that so far the snacks have been pretty good. I'm especially looking forward to the meatloaf that's for dinner tonight—in approximately 108 minutes (not that I'm counting).

At my first week's weigh-in I lost 2.7 pounds. This is very exciting, and by my calculation, exactly 10% of my goal loss. Thank god! I have been absolutely starving at some points during the day, so I'm glad to see this is paying off. This positive reinforcement was particularly important on a Saturday night when we had a dozen party-goers at my house and I had to pretend to be drinking (lest they think I'm pregnant with baby #5 and totally insane) and stick to eating carrot sticks while everyone else munched on nachos and cookies. Ah well, those skinny friends of mine will get fatter and fatter while I will look better and better. All part of my evil master plan. *Mwah ha ha ha!* I thought everyone in North America was obese? Why are all my friends a size 2? I must live in a bad neighbourhood.

I stayed on that plan for about five months and in the end lost the 28 pounds. This was a couple of years ago, and I have allowed about five pounds to sneak back on. I've also increased my exercise schedule, however, so from where I'm sitting (not in size 2s, FYI) it's all looking pretty good. Or at least I thought it was until a male friend saw me in a swimsuit shot and said "Not bad, Kathy. You're no Valerie Bertinelli, but not bad." Sigh.

Signs You Know You Made The Right Choice to Go On Jenny

1. When you tell people you're on Jenny, they say "Good for you" instead of "What, are you crazy? You don't need that!"

2. When your 7-year-old daughter explains to her friends that the reasons Mommy is on diet is because "She looks like she has a baby in her tummy but she doesn't."

3. When you say you'd like to lose 10 pounds by Christmas and people continue to look at you expectantly until you say "and the other 15 by spring."

4. Simply not drinking alcohol and eating junk food has decreased your grocery bill by 50 dollars a week.

Men, Fat, and Math

Our discussion of dieting just wouldn't be complete if we didn't include a word or two about men. Remember back in high school and university? Most of our diets were undertaken in an effort to impress one of these strange creatures. Oh sure, you probably told yourself it was "to fit into that skirt" again, but who were you kidding? The only reason you wanted to wear that skirt again was to look hot at the dance/party/whatever. Because *he* was going to be there. Nailed it, didn't I?

I like to think that we're older and wiser now, and that dieting these days is more about our health than what anyone else thinks. Just in case I've got that wrong, though, check out these statistics. They'll force you to give your head a shake before you start counting calories for anyone's benefit but your own.

According to www.askmen.com, 70% of men, when surveyed, said they wouldn't cheat on their wives, but 52% of these same men said they would leave their wives if their wives got fat. Let's explore that a bit, shall we? Men, you might want to look for protective covering.

1. First off, let's define fat. Some of us have had life-altering experiences that have led us to look the way we currently look. Giving birth to your stupid children, for starters. Or maybe it was just a traumatic experience with the school council regarding the overuse of permanent markers. Anything can set us off. You, in particular, do.

2. Sure, leave us once we're fat and you think no one else will want us. You've been watching way too many sitcoms where the fat guy gets the thin, good-looking girl—*King of Queens, Still Standing,* all the way back to *The Honeymooners* with Ralph & Alice—which brings us to . . .

3. What, so you guys haven't put on weight, either? Oh wait, I'm starting to put this together now. The reason 70% of you wouldn't cheat on your wives is because you're too fat to get anyone else to do it with you. *But,* if you leave your wife, then you'll have time for exercising, living right, and eating better food because you won't have to deal with annoying things like children, domestic duties, and marital obligation. Got it.

Oh, what the hell, ladies, 50% of all marriages end in divorce anyway. It's only a 2% differential we're talking about here. Pass the chips.

And, FYI, Cameron Diaz was *skinny* the last time I looked, and she hasn't been married yet. Sort of supports my theory, don't you think? Or maybe she's just waiting for someone's fat ex-husband to come along.

Conclusion
The Whole Enchilada

If you've managed to work your way through this book, and maybe even try out some of the recipes, I hope you will have discovered what generations of moms have always known: Whether eating in or eating out, having gourmet fare or stovetop macaroni, sacrificing nutrition for flavour or vice versa, all we really need or want is to get out kids to just shut up and eat. They need to stop talking about how bad the cooking is and focus on how good their day was. Or how challenging it was.

Believe it or not, eating together—messy, hurried, harried, and inconvenient though it may be—does have an upside. This all came into focus for me a few years ago, during a unique freelance writing assignment. *Today's Parent* editor Sarah Moore asked me to write a "dinner diary" about the challenges of having a sitdown meal every night with my husband and four children. Strange as it sounds, given my (now well-established) on-again, off-again relationship with the family meal, I was excited.

You see, I was feeling a bit smug. In researching this book, I learned that a huge percentage of families *don't* sit down for a family meal at least once a day. Somehow, though—and despite my other numerous other shortcomings on the parenting front—I do, in fact, manage to get a family dinner on the table at least 4 out of 5 weeknights. Just in case it slipped your mind the last 200 or so pages, let me remind you that I have four children—then ranging in age from 4 to 14, all of whom have their own outside interests and organized sports—and a workaholic husband. Am I wrong to feel a little proud of this dinnertime achievement? Sure, I'll admit that the dinners are sometimes eaten later than we like, or consist of "foods that can be prepared in between the window of driving Victoria to dance and taking Bridget to soccer," but we still manage to mostly pull it off. Given this state of affairs, I figured I needed to warn Sarah. I admitted that while we did have our own eating idiosyncrasies (i.e., most of my children hate my cooking and my husband rarely looks up from his BlackBerry to see what it is that he is putting in his mouth—or what the children are pulling out of theirs—my main concern was that this "tell-all" diary might be a bit, well, boring. *Ha ha ha ha ha ha ha!*

My first decision was to not tell the children about this writing assignment so that they would "be themselves." A word about this odd choice: Normally I am opposed to letting children "be themselves"—it only leads to disgusting social habits and ruined furniture—but for this cause I was willing to take the chance. My second decision was not to tell my husband either. A little sneaky, sure, but if this was to be a true picture of our family dinners (with me coming out looking great, of course!), secrecy had to be maintained.

I'm going to end this exploration of children, chicken, and chardonnay by borrowing from the results of that assignment here, because (1) a lot of people liked it, and (2) I think it sort of sums up how and why eating together as a family is actually something you might want to do.

The Dinner Diary

Day 1

My thought process regarding dinner actually starts at breakfast time, as I mentally run through the day to determine (1) who will be home for dinner, (2) what time we will need to eat, (3) how much time I will need, and (4) when during the day I will be preparing the dinner. This will be a relatively quiet day—no lessons planned and Steve will be home on time tonight. I don't have any meetings in the afternoon, so I'll have time to make the dinner once the kids are home from school. Carte blanche, so to speak. I could make meatloaf, which Steve loves, but two of the kids hate. Or pasta, which three of the kids love, but Steve isn't fond of—or pork tenderloin, which I love but Vicky won't eat. Or I'll do what I usually do: wait until the last minute, see who is annoying me the most by the time I need to make dinner, and cook something they don't like. (What, you think moms don't think this way? Get over yourself.)

After attending a volunteer session at the school, getting two kids out for a haircut, coming home, and refereeing fights for an hour, I decide on the meatloaf. At least one member of the family will be happy. Throw in a cauliflower casserole (don't give me that look, it's good!), steamed carrots, and away we go. All right, add an ice cream pie, which they all will love (and will make me look good for the purposes of the article; I never make dessert). My 14-year-old is amazed and stunned by the ice cream pie, which she automatically zooms in on the moment she comes in the door. "Who made this? You did? But you don't know how to cook!" Lovely.

The GO train is slightly late, but we still sit down to eat at 6:15, which is pretty good for us. Moans about the meatloaf ("There's a waste of a half a cow"), the cooked-ness of the carrots, and the unfairness about making dessert on a night where they surely won't finish their horrible dinner are all normal. As is the sound of humming BlackBerrys (his and mine). The only difference is that he looks at his and answers his emails while I pour juice, wipe faces, and fetch ketchup. Once dinner is over the fight over clearing the table starts (we have a schedule, yet we still fight over the number of dishes I "deliberately" put out on the disfavoured child's night).

Day 2

Tonight's meal will be mostly a function of timing. Bridget, my 7-year-old, has her first soccer practice and game starting at 6:30. My husband normally arrives home at 6:15. We have to eat and get her dressed for the game in that period. Naturally, then, this must be a meal that the kids will eat without too much complaint. However, my two older children, Alex and Victoria, will be out for dinner tonight, so I can't make anything they like or there will be cries of "You always make the stuff we like when we're not here!" As they only "like" about six dishes, I should easily be able to sidestep this particular landmine. I picked up a pot roast in my fly-by visit to the grocery store today, but that would be red meat two days in a row. Pasta is easy and good but the older two actually like that. I think it might be time to pull out the famous baked-bean casserole, which the two little kids like because of its well-known "magical fruit" qualities. Might not make Bridget the most popular kid on the soccer field, but you can't have everything.

All right, in the end I went for the pot roast—no, not to satisfy my beef-hungry husband, but because I left it out on the counter after grocery shopping (something about being called away to wipe a bottom made it slip my mind), and I was afraid that if I didn't cook it the same day it would be wasted. At least the older kids will be happy they missed it. So dinner on the table, four of us there, pushing it down as fast as we can (while the two kids satisfy their inexplicable and constant need to use the washroom during the meal, and for a long period of time, if you know what I mean), so we can make it to the soccer field in time. Add in me yelling, "Don't get ketchup on your soccer uniform" (which Bridget has been wearing since she got home from school), and the ever-humming BlackBerrys, and it is as quiet as can be expected. Until the kids remember the damn leftover ice cream pie, which I knew would come back to haunt me. Serves me right for making nice by making dessert. They cry and cry they won't get any before soccer because they can't finish their meal so I break my #1 dinner rule and let them leave some dinner behind to get to the pie. And away to the soccer field . . .

Day 3

As usual, my thoughts of dinner start first thing in the morning, as I realize that I have promised a friend that I would watch her three children (aged 2, 7, and 11) from 5:00 until 6:00 (oh, that wonderful time of the day when children are at their best!). She needs to head to her job before her husband returns home from his job. I also realize that my own 14-year-old daughter Victoria has a dance class that starts at 5:30, and I have to drive her there. This class has been at this time for the past eight months, so I'm not sure why I totally forgot about this. Oh well, she'll have to get to class early, and then my husband can pick her up at 6:30 on his way home, and we'll eat at 6:45 like we usually do after her dance class—oh crap, just realized something else. (Please bear in mind that all of this is running through my head at 6:03 a.m., before I've even gotten out of bed.) I have 11 women coming to my house at 7:30 for our "Chic Lit" book club. At the past few outings, the appetizers have been worthy of a half-hour cooking special. So dinner will have to be something I can cook with six children on-site, and that can be served, eaten, and cleaned up by no later than 7:00 (time to sweep the popcorn out of the living room and slap some store-bought pâté on a plate). Hmmm. I'm thinking cream of mushroom soup as the sauce. . . .

The cream of mushroom soup did come into play, but I managed to get it on top of sole, a healthy white fish (never mind that I topped the fish with cheddar cheese and onions as well). I managed to simultaneously put the fish together, get the rice into the rice cooker (does saffron still have any effect when it is about six years old? I hate to throw it out as it was so expensive), and run between the kitchen and the family room in an attempt to stop the 2-year-old's tears from flowing as the discovery that Mom will be leaving the building sinks in. I totally ignore anyone over the age of four and trust that if Band-Aids are needed, I will hear about it.

My sister calls en route to the book club and I invite her to dinner, which forces me to spread the fish just a bit thinner in the casserole dish and throw some milk in to stretch the sauce (the biblical fish/loaf story has nothing on me). The surplus children are picked up, the dinner is on the table, husband and daughter walk through the door, and we sit down to eat, all as I'm facing the clock and counting the minutes until the women arrive—but not my sister as she's stuck in traffic and I have her plate wrapped in foil and sitting on the stove. The kids fight over who gets to sit next to Auntie Margaret (with me screaming "She's not even here yet!") and anything and everything else at the table. A side note: I thought fish was supposed to make you smarter, but my kids are pushing aside the browned onions covered with cheese. Who doesn't like onions covered with baked cheese? I know my thighs are screaming "we love it!" Come to think of it, I'm not so sure this has done much for my brain cells either, as I realize that I have broken the cardinal rule of cooking before company comes over and now have to somehow combat the lingering smell of fish in the air. I'll just serve lots of wine. I leave the messy table and wish my husband farewell and good luck in his quest to corral the children through table clearing, homework, baths, books, and bedtime. My work here is done.

Day 4

"Do you think we should have ham for dinner tonight?" I ask my 7-year-old and 4-year-old at our Burger King lunch. "Can I get a crown?" is their answer. Ham would work tonight. While we don't have any outside commitments after dinner, my husband is stopping for drinks after work ("But I'll still be on the regular train"; uh-huh), and it can be served stone cold. I was toying with keeping the ham for tomorrow night but my son Alex, who *looooves* ham, won't be home for dinner tomorrow and right now I like him so I'll move things around. Ham it is—and one of the great things about it is that I can usually get the kids to eat it all up in one meal (to avoid leftovers) merely by whispering two small words: "Ham cakes." You don't want to know. I do, however, expect to regret the decision to be nice to my son once he announces (as he surely will) to his wannabe vegan older sister that we are eating a pig. She knows this intellectually and chooses not to acknowledge it, a choice I support.

So I go with the ham, but I make a choice to serve the dinner "buffet" style, which in our house means that the kids are allowed to choose what they want, but if they don't at least have an adequate sample of each dish, there is no dessert and no snacks later on.

Nicholas, age 4, eats everything and revels in dessert. Bridget, age 7, eats everything and chows down on cookies. Alexander, age 12, turns up an hour late from his road hockey game and as punishment is forced to eat the huge portions that I piled on his plate while the dishes were still warm. Victoria, age 14, eats three buns and whines all night about how starving she is. Steve, age 41, has a small dinner ("big lunch, sorry") and then dives into the freezer for that last piece of the flippin' ice cream pie. And they're gone.

Day 5

Chicken quesadillas. This is my plan at 8:30 a.m. We'll see how it goes, as the kids all enjoy this and right now they are not pissing me off. They are absent, but they're not pissing me off. This is an unusual day, though, as my husband Steve has taken the day off to attend Nicky's field trip to a local farm. I predict that by noon Steve will be pining for his nice, quiet, orderly office on Bay Street. The field trip ends at noon, which means that I will have that dreaded creature—"The husband with the afternoon off"—upsetting my regular routine and generally getting underfoot. Dinner may take a twist.

Okay, 5:30 and I still haven't made a move toward getting dinner on the table, so the takeout menus are spread out (this is my most used "cookbook") and we decide that Swiss Chalet is on tap—at least I've stuck with the basic "chicken" theme. As Bridget goes around the table stealing everyone's skin (off their chicken, that is), there is no question that this meal is a hit. Steve and Victoria barely look up from their sauce dipping to contribute to the scintillating debate over whether Alexander's hair is cool and gnarly or simply makes him look like a homeless person (alarmingly, it seems that either look is okay with him). Cleanup is easy, but I am on the hook for the quesadillas tomorrow night, as the kids have an amazing memory for the times I promise a "good" meal.

Day 6

You guessed it—the chicken. This will have to be made in between entertaining a family of four for lunch (which lasts until 5:00), driving one daughter to ballet, picking up one son from the GO station and depositing him at a birthday party, and then returning to the party to drive him home. This is a weekend and we're still scheduling dinner "in between." The quesadillas are mostly a hit, except for Bridget, whom, while claiming she loves chicken quesadillas, takes all the chicken out. She is advised by her brother to "drown the real flavour" with a mixture of ketchup, BBQ sauce, and sour cream. She does. More wine. Another family meal prepared, presented, evaluated, consumed, and dismissed. Tomorrow we are surprisingly invited out for a meal, so for one night the pressure is off me—except when it comes to monitoring the children's table manners. And then next week the whole cycle starts again.

So that was it, really. No major disasters, a couple of successes, and generally a typical week *chez moi*. The moral of the story? Should we expect our family mealtime to resemble the cheerful, respectful, and communicable tableaus presented by *Leave It to Beaver* and other shows featuring an idealized version of family life? Not at all. But what we should expect, and do receive, is that very valuable gift known in the business world as "face time." In the midst of our busy lives (which we, for the most part, chose), it is only by putting ourselves in front of our children (hopefully out of the range of flying peas and insults) that we can really start to understand and appreciate the day-to-day adventures each of us has—for good or for bad. Are the meals appreciate and enjoyed? Not always. Are they perfectly balanced, nutritious, and wholesome? Maybe sometimes. Do we have inspiring and knowledgeable dinner conversations? Hardly ever. I suspect the few times we were getting close might have been thrown off track by flatulence humour.

Sometimes it is absolutely true that the whole is greater than the sum of its parts. Apart, we can be kind of messy—running here and there, poking, kicking, yelling, checking BlackBerrys and daydreaming about pedicures—but together, well, together,

it's an entirely different picture. Together, we talk: about hair-
cuts and school assignments, about dance lessons and book
clubs, about field trips and friends and what that stain on Nic's
pants might actually be. We fight: about who sits where and why
Alexander is looking at him that way and who is farting and why
it's JUST NOT FAIR. It's not perfect, and it's not even always
pleasant, but it's our life as a family. And at our house (and, I expect, yours) the whole family is definitely greater (and sometimes grosser) than its individual (and sometimes disgusting)
parts.

Now pass the wine, sit down, and—really—shut up and eat.

Appendix
You Are Not Alone.
Q and A from Other Frustrated Moms

In my life, I'm lucky enough to meet many different moms, from many different places, with children of varying ages, backgrounds, and temperaments. Despite this range, many of them have the same food challenges when it comes to their children. I thought I'd dip into my "mailbag" (oh, okay, my Twitter account) and share some of their questions with you—plus my own insightful responses, of course.

Q: What is a Supertaster?
A: Dear SuperMom: Supertaster is a term that came into popular use in the early 1990s, when an experimental scientist (and no doubt a picky eater herself) discovered that some people had taste buds that were supersensitive to strong and bitter tastes. Picky eaters are not necessarily Supertasters, and vice versa. This scientist estimates that 25% of the population are Supertasters. And I say, so what? If you have four children, one out of the four

is apparently going to be a pain in the ass at the dinner table. No kidding. Take my advice and stop at three kids. If you already have a Supertaster, well, what the hell, you may as well keep going. I believe that I myself belong to a little-known group called the *SuperWasters*. I can't seem to stop spending money on perfectly good fruits and vegetables that inevitably get thrown into the garbage because my picky children won't eat them.

Q. My son won't eat vegetables, meat, or try anything new. Should I be worried he'll get scurvy?
A: Dear Captain Bligh: Scurvy results from a lack of vitamin C, and has traditionally been a common disease of sailors, pirates, and people lost on the Blue Lagoon. As long as your son is getting vitamin C through his Flintstone vitamins, fruit chews "with REAL vitamin C," or a big glass of OJ every day, he should be fine. But check with your doctor. And FYI—last time I checked, there was no vitamin C in meat. Perhaps your son is a Supertaster.

Q: My daughter eats cold hot dogs, bologna, and Braun-schweiger for breakfast. Is this okay?
A: Dear Fraulein: If I knew what the hell Braunschweiger was, I could answer this question. Never mind—just looked it up. It's a meaty pâté type of thing—and get this—loaded with vitamin A, iron, and proteins. So if you can get past the idea of spreading meat first thing in the morning, I say go for it. In terms of the hot dogs and bologna, I cover non-traditional breakfast foods in another part of the book. Just as we've had to adapt ourselves out of the established nine-to-five, Monday-to-Friday workweek, I really do believe it's time to shake up what we believe should be served at each meal. Let her have the Braunschweiger. Could be worse—she could be a Supertasting pirate.

Q: My son eats only five foods: bread, bananas, pasta, milk, potatoes, chicken nuggets, and apple juice. What can I do to change this?

A: **Dear Beautiful Mind**: I wouldn't worry about it as much as I would worry about the times you've been helping your son with his math homework. By my calculation, and your own admission, he is actually eating *seven* different types of food—many more, in fact, if one counts each type of pasta as a separate food. Unless he is one of those kids who can only eat one type of pasta *even though they all taste the same.* . . . Anyway, look at the food choices he's making! Miraculously, he's hitting all five food groups, so you're off to a good start. Sometimes children get stuck with certain foods because of a label they are comfortable with. Start telling him pork is a "new chicken" and that rice is just small potatoes. Jessica Seinfeld's got nothing on *my* deceptive cooking. Maybe you and Braunschweiger lady can get the kids together for a meat-spread sandwich brunch.

Q: My son just ate the wrapper on his muffin. Was this just to piss me off?

A: **Dear Angry Lady**: Yes. It is a basic way of life for children. Next question.

Q: Why can't different foods touch on your plate?

A: **Dear Obvious**: Um, because food is normally an inanimate object and is not able to move from one location to another. Unless it's horribly undercooked fish or runny Jell-O on a pitching boat. Oh, wait, you mean you have a child who won't let foods be placed on his plate in a way that might accidentally lead to the foods coming into contact with another type of food. While

I'll admit I'm not crazy about my Braunschweiger getting mixed up with my muffin wrappers, the easy solution is to invest in some fondue plates, which are sectioned off. And then you can enjoy the fondue section of my book as well.

Q: Why is it okay to try strange-looking candy but not strange-looking vegetables?
A: Dear Strang'R: I assume you are talking about your children. I'm not sure why children have a highly developed candy detector, but the fact of the matter is that they do. Instead of focusing on making new and different types of food snacks, our food manufacturers need to start repackaging vegetables in brightly coloured wrappers and creating superheroes that look like pieces of broccoli. Think about it! If we could have bought little prepackaged bits of celery that could be stripped down and turned into surfers long before the cheese-string people came up with this, we would have stood a chance of getting the little buggers to eat it. As it stands, we've lost the initiative. In fact, the dairy people have been ahead of the fruit and vegetable people for a long time. Yogurt tastes better in a tube, cheese tastes better in a string, and milk tastes better when mixed with a thick chocolate syrup. And let's face it, going the other way and trying to make candy taste bad doesn't work: Think about Thrills gum.

Q: My 2-year-old goes on food strikes. All she wants is milk or tofu dogs or Bear Paw cookies. Should I be worried?
A: Dear Ms. Hoffa: I'd be worried about any 2-year-old who eats tofu dogs of her own free will.

Q: Why do kids want ketchup on everything?
A: **Dear Soul Mate**: Because we are bad cooks. And ketchup makes everything taste like it came through a drive-thru window.

Q: Why can't I walk past an open bottle of wine?
A: **Dear Soul Mate II**: Why should you?

Q: How do I keep my 9-year-old twins seated through an entire meal?
A: **Dear Mrs. Ants in Their Pants**: A couple of my children suffered from this ailment, too. At first I thought they were jumping up to get away from the questionable meals that I put in front of them, but I've come to realize that they do this with every meal—even the *good* ones (i.e., the fast food takeout ones). I used to spend a lot of time setting the table before my children got there. Now, recognizing their need to get up and down, I have them make themselves useful when they're up and fetch napkins, glasses, ketchup, etc. I am also a fan of duct tape.

Q: Why does my family insist on planning dinner when we haven't even finished lunch?
A: **Dear Nostradamus**: My children also have this annoying habit. They don't seem to understand that after cooking dinner about 18,473 times, I'm just not as into it as I used to be. This is why the answer of "something nasty" has become standard when I'm asked that cringe-inducing question, "What's for dinner?", particularly when it crops up during the waning stages of lunch. Which they also hated.

Q: Do other people fantasize about killing someone just to get their Cinnabon?
A: **Dear Nice Lady**: I don't ever eat them. Please don't come to my house. I'm moving anyway.

Q: How do my kids know they don't like something if they haven't even tasted it yet?
A: **Dear Soul Mate III**: Because we aren't the world's greatest cooks and they have some history with the "Mommy tried a new food experiment today!" approach to dinner. I have to admit that this drives me crazy as well, so I have taken to a little bit of treachery. When my offspring sit down and say, "Mom, have I had this? Do I like it?" I answer "You love it! That's why I made it again." Reality is they've never had anything like it before—and probably won't again. Sometimes I tell them they *can't* have something—that it's just for Mom and Dad. That usually makes them insist on trying it. If all else fails, get out the ketchup and hot sauce and tell them to (literally if not figuratively) suck it up.

Q: Is there any other food besides chicken and beef that constitutes the main part of any meal?
A: **Dear Farmer Sue**: Not sure why we all fall back on this tradition of a protein (meat, chicken), one or two vegetables, and a starch (potato, rice, bread). At my house, I try to mix it up. Sometimes I go crazy and serve three vegetables and no starch, or two different types of meat (ever heard of mixed grill, kids?). Funnily enough, it's my husband who seems totally thrown off by this. "Where are the potatoes?" he'll ask, using his best whiny voice. I say as long as they can fill their plates, it's a meal. This is

why I am the queen of leftovers and buffets. The only other option is to investigate tofu. Which I advise against.

Q: Why is it when I call my teenage daughter to dinner she comes in, sits in "her spot" without saying a word, and doesn't offer to help at all while I race around trying to get dinner on the table?

A: **Dear Funny Lady**: Didn't you just say she was a teenager? In all likelihood the only conversation you're going to get out of her is a mumbled, "Why is dinner so late tonight?" or "Does it have to be so gross?" And honestly, why should she help you? Do you do *anything* at all to help her?

Q: Why does my husband sit down at the table and then jump up right when dinner is served to get a glass of wine/pepper/go to the boys room/etc., every single time?

A: **Dear Mrs. Bounce**: Most men are unaware of any of their surroundings. They are simple creatures. It's not until you put the food in front of your husband that his brain will register that he is actually about to eat. Armed with this knowledge, his thought process then turns to the next activity he is about to undertake. *Wait, I need a drink. Wait, if I don't go pee now I'll need to right in the middle of this steak. Wait, I'd better get some seasoning because she never cooks it the way I like it.* Men also have trouble with the end of the meal. They don't seem to realize that this is, in fact, a signal to get up and help clear the table. A cattle prod is useful. It is curious how a male child can go from not being able to sit down at the table to a grown man who can't get up at the end.

Q: Why does my child insist on using his shirt—neck or sleeve—as a napkin?

A: Dear Enviro-girl: My children often do this as well, and while it used to drive me crazy, I have had them adapt to at least wiping the food on the inside of their shirts, so that (1) they don't look messy the next time we go out, and (2) the accumulated crust inside their shirt is sure to (eventually) bother them enough to actually change that mangy T-shirt, which has stains on the outside as well. In my mind, if they wear the same shirt for two to three days, we're doing our part for the environment, and for my laundry efforts as well. Win/win. You might, however, make a concerted effort to get them out of this habit prior to seeking gainful employment.

Q: How is it that my teenage son can have perfect hand–eye co-ordination on the volleyball court and golf course, yet when it comes to pouring juice, half of it ends up on the counter?

A: Dear Apple: Don't tell me you weren't like this as a boy. Just like men never know how big a piece of cake to cut, or how to make sure everyone gets the same amount of Smarties in the car, males have an issue with judging space and distance. This also explains why your 12 inches is different than ours.

Q: Is it a bad idea to let your children watch TV while they are eating dinner?

A: Dear Oprah: I usually try to gauge what the reaction will be to dinner before I allow the kitchen television to be turned on. If the meal is something they really don't want to eat, television can be a good distraction. Also, I find that children are just as bad at multi-tasking as men, so if you want your kids to sit longer at the kitchen table, go ahead and fire up the tube. They will often stare at the screen with fork held midway between plate and lips. On the other hand, you may not want them to stick around longer, or you might actually want to engage them in discussion (see Chapter 4 for my highly successful conversational game of Roses and Thorns). Allow one night a week with television, for a treat, but only if it's when my show (*Birth Days*—check your local listings) is on.

Q: Should you force your child to eat the last few bites on their plate, or are you pushing them to eat when they're not hungry, thus contributing to a possible overeating or obesity problem?
A: **Dear Slim**: I find the best way to avoid this problem is to allow the children to put the portion they want on their plate. You, as the parent, can have veto power to say it's not a full plate, but they have to have a little bit of something (and okay, fine, the items don't have to touch each other). Don't make them finish, but there's no dessert (*yes, it's a bribe, get over yourself*) unless they do.

Q: Is it okay to stick a fork in my husband's hand because his chewing is too loud?
A: **Dear Nice Calm Lady**: Yes. Better than in his neck.

Q: Why is it when I make "kid food" (e.g., Hamburger Helper, Kraft Dinner), my husband is the only one who truly enjoys it?
A: **Dear Naïve Lady**: Look for my next book, *Why Men Are More Children Than Children Are Children*. Failing that, perhaps his Mom

was a mean old lady who never let him experience a real child-hood. Either works for me.

Q: Why did my husband not like salmon for years and then suddenly decide to like it, after I asked you to re-arrange your dinner party menu for him?
A: Dear Friend: Because men don't know what they like and what they don't like. You must have forgotten to tell him he liked it.

Q: My son once barfed after eating a banana (due to the flu), but he hasn't touched a banana since. How do I convince him that he's not allergic to bananas?
A: Dear Monkey's Aunt: Not sure on the banana thing, but I'm thinking it might be a good strategy to force your kids to vomit after having French fries or pizza. Personally, I've thrown up after drinking wine and I'm pretty sure that's an allergic reaction also. He could be right.

Q: Why will children eat virtually any meat as long as we say it is chicken?
A: Dear Einstein: They're not that smart. That's why they should just shut up and eat.